Tourism Research in China

TOURISM ESSENTIALS

Series Editors: Chris Cooper, *Oxford Brookes University, UK*, C. Michael Hall, *University of Canterbury, New Zealand* and Dallen J. Timothy, *Arizona State University, USA*

Tourism Essentials is a dynamic new book series of short accessible volumes focusing on a specific area of tourism studies. It aims to present cutting-edge research on significant and emerging topics in tourism, providing a concise overview of the field as well as examining the key issues and future research possibilities. This series aims to create a new generation of tourism authors by encouraging young researchers as well as more established academics. The books will provide insight into the latest perspectives in tourism studies and will be an essential resource for postgraduate students and researchers.

Full details of all the books in this series and of all our other publications can be found on http://www.channelviewpublications.com, or by writing to Channel View Publications, St. Nicholas House, 31–34 High Street, Bristol BS1 2AW, UK.

TOURISM ESSENTIALS: 3

Tourism Research in China

Themes and Issues

Songshan (Sam) Huang and Ganghua Chen

CHANNEL VIEW PUBLICATIONS
Bristol • Buffalo • Toronto

Library of Congress Cataloging in Publication Data
Huang, Songshan.
Tourism Research in China: Themes and Issues/Songshan (Sam) Huang and Ganghua Chen.
Tourism Essentials: 3
Includes bibliographical references and index.
1. Tourism—Research—China. I. Chen, Ganghua. II. Title.
G155.8.C6H83 2015
338.4'79151–dc23 2015019502

British Library Cataloguing in Publication Data
A catalogue entry for this book is available from the British Library.

ISBN-13: 978-1-84541-547-1 (hbk)
ISBN-13: 978-1-84541-546-4 (pbk)

Channel View Publications
UK: St. Nicholas House, 31–34 High Street, Bristol BS1 2AW, UK.
USA: UTP, 2250 Military Road, Tonawanda, NY 14150, USA.
Canada: UTP, 5201 Dufferin Street, North York, Ontario M3H 5T8, Canada.

Website: www.channelviewpublications.com
Twitter: Channel_View
Facebook: https://www.facebook.com/channelviewpublications
Blog: www.channelviewpublications.wordpress.com

The policy of Multilingual Matters/Channel View Publications is to use papers that are natural, renewable and recyclable products, made from wood grown in sustainable forests. In the manufacturing process of our books, and to further support our policy, preference is given to printers that have FSC and PEFC Chain of Custody certification. The FSC and/or PEFC logos will appear on those books where full certification has been granted to the printer concerned.

Typeset by Techset Composition India (P) Ltd, Bangalore and Chennai, India.

Contents

Figures and Tables

Figures

Tables

Preface

This book provides a selective review of tourism research in China. We intend to offer our readers insights into, and fine-grained analyses of, topics which we have been researching for years and in which we can thus claim a measure of expertise. The book contributes to the sum of tourism scholarship – alongside other scholarly books on China tourism – in its unique positioning which aims to reveal the current state of tourism research in China in selected research areas. China has a distinctive research tradition and tourism researchers in China are subject to the influences of such a tradition. Researchers in China tend to apply their own institutionalised lenses and paradigmatic approaches in studying tourism and tourism-related social and economic phenomena. Although the tourism research community in China is relatively large in terms of the number of researchers, only a small number of tourism researchers in China are able to publish their research output in English in international academic journals. Most of the tourism research output produced in China is published in Chinese academic journals and thus remains inaccessible to researchers in the international research community who cannot read Chinese. There therefore exists a form of information asymmetry between tourism researchers in China and their international counterparts outside China. Whereas tourism researchers in China can mostly read and access tourism literature in English produced by the international tourism research community, the reverse is not the case. Many researchers outside China cannot easily access the tourism literature created in China in the Chinese language.

Such an issue was actually flagged in some email exchanges on the Tourism Research Information Network (TRINET), an international tourism research community listserv group managed by the School of Travel Industry Management, University of Hawaii. A few TRINET members highlighted the need to 'dig out' those 'hidden gems' of tourism scholarship in languages other than English. Unfortunately, several years passed, and not much has been done to reveal the 'hidden gems'.

This book may lay claim to being one of the few academic attempts to reveal these 'hidden gems' to the international tourism research community. Considering the preponderance of China tourism in the world and the increasing importance of China tourism research for tourism scholarship, perhaps it is needed even more urgently!

There are more hot topics in relation to China tourism that warrant being covered in the book but were not. These include the outbound tourism market from China, smart technology and tourism, the impact of social media on tourism, city and urban tourism, heritage and cultal tourism, red tourism, to name just a few. We look forward to seeing these topics covered in future books of this type.

We take this opportunity to thank the commissioning editor Ms Elinor Robertson and her team for their support, understanding and patience in this book's manuscript writing and preparation process. It has always been a pleasure to see Elinor and her dedicated team at different tourism conferences. Our appreciation goes to the Tourism Essentials series editors, Prof Chris Cooper (Oxford Brookes University, UK), Prof C. Michael Hall (University of Canterbury, Christchurch, New Zealand) and Prof Dallen J. Timothy (Arizona State University, USA), for providing such a book series platform to present worthy academic works. We thank the series editors and the reviewer for their encouraging, constructive and thoughtful comments on the proposal of this book.

We acknowledge the institutional support we received from the University of South Australia Business School and the School of Tourism Management, Sun Yat-sen University. Special thanks are given to those colleagues around us who show understanding, emotional support, and collegiality toward our work in our hectic academic life.

Finally, we would wish to express our gratitude to our spouses, Amy (Sam's wife) and Meidan (Ganghua's wife) for their tolerance, love and support in enabling our work. Life wouldn't be as rewarding without their good company!

Songshan (Sam) Huang
Ganghua Chen
April 2015

1 The Landscape of Tourism Research in China: An Overview

Introduction

Tourism research in China did not start until the end of the 1970s, when tourism development was encouraged by central government policies (Zhang, 2003). Tourism research has also developed in higher education institutes in China through the establishment of tourism programmes in universities (Huang, 2001). In 1979, in order to meet the industry's need for more specialised tourism service staff, the first tourism higher learning institute – Shanghai Tourism College – was established under the auspices of the China National Tourism Administration (CNTA), marking the beginning of China tourism higher education. In the following years CNTA collaborated with eight universities (e.g. Nankai University, Sun Yat-sen University, Northwest University and Hangzhou University) across the country to set up tourism undergraduate and postgraduate degree programmes (Huang, 2001). With over 30 years of development, China's tourism higher education has developed on a significant scale. According to the CNTA (2014), by the end of 2013 there were 544 universities providing tourism undergraduate degree (BA or equivalent) programmes and around 194,200 students enrolled in these programmes. At postgraduate level, there were 4300 students enrolled in postgraduate research masters (coursework plus thesis component) programmes and 800 enrolled in tourism-related PhD programmes. In addition, a total of 1067 universities had tertiary tourism diploma or associate degree (2–3 years) programmes with an enrolment of around 366,800 students in 2013 (CNTA, 2014). According to the China Tourism Education Association

(2012), by the end of 2011 there were at least 1100 supervisors for masters students and about 90 supervisors for doctoral students in tourism programmes. In China only qualified researchers (usually at associate professor and professor levels) can supervise masters or doctoral students (Bao *et al.*, 2014), so the masters and doctoral student supervisors may provide a good representation for the number of active researchers on the faculties of Chinese universities.

Tourism higher education on this massive scale provides the basis for tourism research in China; however, as noted by some scholars (e.g. Zhang, 2003), tourism research has also been rendered by multiple institutions, and agencies and universities are just one of the many types of institutions involved in tourism research in China. Apart from some occasional papers and book chapters introducing and describing the terrain of tourism research in China (e.g. Bao *et al.*, 2014; Hsu *et al.*, 2010; Huang & Hsu, 2008; Ryan & Huang, 2013b; Zhang, 2003) to researchers outside China, especially those who cannot access the Chinese literature, the overall picture of tourism research in China remains blurred. This chapter provides an overview of China's tourism research. In so doing, the chapter also serves to provide fine-grained background information for readers to better understand the various issues covered in other chapters. Issues reviewed in this chapter include researchers, research institutions in China, tourism research themes and topics in China, methods and methodology. At the end of the introductory chapter, we also provide a brief preview of the chapters that follow.

Tourism Researchers in China

Tourism researchers in China are based in different types of institutions. Zhang (2003) classified the institutions and organisations involved in tourism research into the following six categories:

- government agencies;
- government-funded research institutes;
- universities;
- non-governmental organisations (mainly industry associations);
- industry (enterprises); and
- international organisations.

Among these different types of organisations, government bodies, government-funded research institutes and universities are believed to provide more academic research than the other three types of organisations and accordingly host more active researchers. The CNTA is the central government agency in charge of tourism in China. The CNTA formulates tourism policies and oversees the implementation of tourism polices in China. It also takes responsibility for promoting China's destination image among international tourist source markets, organising and implementing industry training and personnel certification. In its internal organisational structure, the CNTA has a department of policy and regulation and this department is closely engaged in tourism policy research at the national level. At the provincial and sub-provincial levels, tourism administrative bodies are commonly established as the government agencies taking charge of tourism development issues. Officers from the CNTA and provincial tourism administrations are expected to publish research, mostly in the form of opinion pieces, in publication outlets such as the *China Tourism News*, an official tourism industry newspaper affiliated to the CNTA itself. In the early 1990s many CNTA and provincial tourism officials published articles in the leading tourism research journal of the time, *Tourism Tribune*, and proved themselves to be a significant cohort of authors influencing tourism research in China (Huang & Hsu, 2008). Tourism officials mainly write articles based on the intellectual work they undertake in association with their office roles, addressing practical industry management and development issues. They rarely refer to research done by university-based researchers and the articles authored by government officials are heavily influenced by mainstream political and policy discourses.

In the government-funded research institutes, tourism research is undertaken at both the Chinese Academy of Social Sciences (CASS) and the Chinese Academy of Sciences (CAS), China's national research institutes specialising in the social sciences and the natural sciences, respectively. In 2000 CASS set up a tourism research centre under its Institute of Finance and Trade Economics (now the National Academy of Economic Strategy, CASS), in response to the central government's call to make tourism a pillar industry in the national economy (Zhang, 2003). The tourism research centre (also the Research Division for Tourism and Leisure) at CASS hosts a number of full-time researchers and receives funding from a private industry group to conduct independent tourism research (Zhang, 2003). Other CASS-affiliated institutes include the Institutes of Economics, Rural Development, Urban Development, History and Sociology, which also host researchers undertaking tourism-related studies (Zhang, 2003).

As most of the tourism resources are nature-based, CAS undertook many tourism planning projects in the early days of tourism development in the 1980s and 1990s. Accordingly, a substantial amount of tourism research output was produced by CAS, mostly through its Institute of Geographic Sciences and Natural Resources Research (Huang & Hsu, 2008; Zhang, 2003).

In June 2008 the CNTA set up its specialised research arm, the China Tourism Academy (CTA). As a statutory research agency directly affiliated to the CNTA, the CTA has four research institutes, namely the Institutes of Tourism Policy and Strategy Studies, the Institute of Tourism Industry and Enterprise Development, the Institute of Regional Tourism Planning and Development, the Institute of International Tourism Development, plus a number of collaborative research centres with some universities (see http:// www.ctaweb.org). It currently employs around 30 full-time researchers who hold PhD degrees in relevant disciplines such as management, economics, geography or ethnology.

It should be noted that researchers at government-funded research institutes like CASS, CAS and CTA carry out their full-time work as research fellows on a different basis. Unlike university-based researchers, they don't undertake teaching as a normal part of work except for supervising research students. On the other hand, as these research institutes receive government funding, the research activities undertaken by their researchers are determined by government research concerns and are directed by government policy research agendas. As a result, researchers based in government-funded research institutes are less independent in selecting their research topics and activities than university-based researchers.

Researchers in Chinese universities are the major constituents of the tourism research community in China. These researchers seem to be more institutionalised in the Chinese higher education system than those researchers stationed in government agencies and government-funded research institutes. To most of them, teaching is a prescribed job expectation in parallel with research. Pure research positions in Chinese universities are not common. Those who do not teach are usually senior academics who take university leadership roles or are heavily involved in administrative responsibilities.

University academics in China, especially junior academics, are not paid as well as academics in Western countries. It is not unusual to see university academics in China taking extra paid work in the industry in addition to their salary from the university. Many tourism academics would also like to take on planning projects or consultancy projects from the industry in order to subsidise their relatively low-paid jobs. Such extra work from outside the university could be a major source of income for tourism academics and some academics may become relatively wealthy through taking on such external work. In most cases, planning projects are industry-oriented and are prescribed to resolve practical development issues at a particular destination. Although some good case studies with clearly defined research problems might be published from data collected from planning projects, in reality very few research articles are generated from tourism planning projects. Nevertheless, tourism academics in China should be acknowledged for their contribution to the development of the tourism industry in China through their involvement in regional tourism planning and the preparation of hotel benchmarking policies (Bao *et al.*, 2014; Zhong *et al.*, 2013).

Very few studies have been undertaken profiling tourism researchers in China. Huang and Hsu (2008), on the basis of author information from 500 research articles published in *Tourism Tribune* from 2000 to 2005, found that the number of male authors was nearly double the number of female authors, and the authors' ages ranged from 21 to 82 with a mean of 37.8 years. Among the 604 authors, 23.5% had a doctoral degree, 22.5% were doctoral students and 30.0% were masters students at the time of publishing their articles. Of the authors, 55.5% were university faculty members, while 30.7% were students, 9.4% were government officials and 3.6% were industry practitioners. In a later study reviewing 1511 research articles published in *Tourism Tribune* and *Tourism Science* from 2000 to 2008, conducted by Hsu *et al.* (2010), it was found that the percentage of female researchers in the younger age groups was progressively increasing. Recently, Bao *et al.* (2014) explored the motivations for choosing tourism research among a small number of early-generation tourism scholars in China who started their tourism research studies in the 1980s. The reasons identified by these pioneer tourism researchers for picking tourism as their dedicated research field included both the need for teaching, faculty development and personal interests, as well as the need for an academic career. Somehow these reasons do not seem to be any different from those identified with forerunner tourism academics outside China (e.g. Pearce, 2011; Pizam, 2011).

The Research Institution (System) in China

China has a very different political establishment from that of Western countries. Certainly, researchers' activities and behaviours tend to be institutionalised in the specific political environment. Except for a small number of scholars (e.g. Bao, 2009; Chen & Bao, 2011), very few tourism researchers in China seem to be reflective of, or even aware of, the institutional constraints they face in conducting tourism research (Huang, 2012; Ryan & Huang, 2013a).

There are many institutional factors that may affect researchers' behaviour, including the research activities they undertake and the research topics they choose to work on. These factors include the national or provincial research funding system, university research incentives, the quality evaluation of research, research resources allocation in universities, and so on. At the central government level in China there are two types of national grants open to researchers: the National Social Sciences Foundation of China (NSSFC) and the National Natural Science Foundation of China (NSFC) grants. The NSSFC grants are administered by the National Planning Office of Philosophy and Social Science, while the NSFC grants are managed by the Foundation itself. Both types of grants have subcategories classified in their systems. As tourism research covers both natural science and social science issues, tourism researchers can apply for grants from both foundations. It is not uncommon to see a researcher obtaining both types of grant, as demonstrated in her/his curriculum vitae. Generally, the funding amount per project from NSFC is larger than from NSSFC.

Other national-level grants include those provided by the Ministry of Education, Ministry of Science and Technology and other central government agencies. In recent years, CNTA has also set up a grant system that is in effect managed by its research arm, the CTA. About 20 grants, ranging from RMB 30,000 to RMB 50,000 are awarded to researchers or research teams each year; most of the awardees are researchers based in universities.

Apart from national-level grants, tourism researchers in China can also apply for grants awarded by provincial or local-level governments. Grants from the industry are also encouraged in the university system and researchers are generally given more flexibility in dealing with industry grants than government-source grants.

Zhu *et al.* (2011) examined the tourism-related grant projects funded by both NSFC and NSSFC from 1987 to 2010. The findings indicate that the tourism-related projects funded by NSFC are mainly in earth sciences (80 projects) and management science (23 projects); tourism impacts, tourism development and tourist behaviours are the main topics addressed in these projects. On the other hand, the tourism projects funded by NSSFC are mainly in applied economics (60 projects), and most of these projects focus on topics like sustainable development, development and protection, and potential and competitiveness. Zhu *et al.* (2011) also found that the topic selection in these projects indicated a trend of *de-tourismisation*, that is, using theories and theoretical frameworks from other disciplines to study the theoretical issues in tourism.

Tourism researchers may still feel that they are disadvantaged as a research community in China's higher education system in comparison with researchers in the more established academic disciplines. In China's current higher education system, tourism management is listed as a secondary disciplinary field under the primary discipline of business administration, which itself is affiliated to management, as one of the 12 discipline clusters (Hu &

Huang, 2011). Most tourism researchers need to rely on a more established disciplinary stronghold (e.g. geography under earth sciences) to compete for grant support. The relatively weak disciplinary position of tourism programmes in China's higher education system (Hu & Huang, 2011) may explain why many tourism researchers would like to de-emphasise tourism in their NSFC and NSSFC grant applications.

Just like in Western countries such as the UK and Australia (Huang, 2011), research has been increasingly subject to state institutional surveillance in China. Many universities, especially those which are research-oriented, would have internal quality journal metrics to evaluate faculty publications. Among Chinese academic journals, the *Beijing University Core Journals*, and those sourced by the *Science Citation Index* (SCI) and the *China Social Science Citation Index* (CSSCI) are generally regarded as more prestigious than other journals in publication evaluation. In recent years, an increasing number of Chinese universities has started to encourage their academic staff to publish in international English academic journals. SCI and SSCI journals are valued more than others and journal impact factors are also among the common indices in staff publication evaluation. Internal publication incentives are instituted in many universities and it is not unusual to see monetary incentives, which with a high-ranked journal publication could go as high as RMB 100,000 (around US$16,130 at current exchange rates). Certainly, such publication incentive arrangements will be among the driving forces that change tourism research in China.

Research Themes and Topics

Many studies have set out to describe tourism research in China in terms of research themes and topics. These include those published in English (e.g. Bao *et al.*, 2014; Hsu *et al.*, 2010; Huang & Hsu, 2008), and in Chinese (e.g. Wu *et al.*, 2001; Zhang *et al.*, 2013). Generally, tourism researchers in China seem to attend more to tourism attraction and resources development, planning issues and macro-industry management issues in their research topic selection. Micro business management and marketing issues are less common. Table 1.1 lists the research themes/topics identified in four review studies. Among these studies, Zhang *et al.*'s (2013) study seems to be most comprehensive in its review scope. This study included 16,024 tourism-related research articles collected from three major academic databases from 2003 to 2012 in its analysis. The authors referred to the national standard, *Academic Disciplines Classification and Codes* (GB/T 13745-2009), in clustering the themes. It was found that tourism geography, tourism development of

Table 1.1 Research themes in four studies

	Study I	Study II	Study III	Study IV
Author (publication year)	Bao et al. (2014)	Huang & Hsu (2008)	Hsu et al. (2010)	Zhang et al. (2013)
Publication outlet and language	*Annals of Tourism Research*/English	*International Journal of Tourism and Hospitality Administration*/English	Book chapter in *Tourism Research: A 20-20 Vision*/ English	*Tourism Tribune*/Chinese
Scope of review	Four Chinese tourism journals (2005–2010): *Tourism Tribune; Tourism Forum; Journal of BISU'; Tourism Science.*	*Tourism Tribune* (2000–2005).	Two Chinese tourism journals (2000–2008): *Tourism Tribune; Tourism Science.*	Chinese core journals database; CSSCI database; and Chinese Science Citation Database (CSCD) (2003–2012).
Themes identified	• Tourist/visitor studies (12.4%); • Economic issues (10%); • Tourism impacts (9.8%); • Destinations (9.3%); • Cultural tourism (8.5%); • Research methods and issues (8.2%); • Sustainable development issues (4.7%);	• Tourism attraction/ resources/product development, management and protection (11.8%); • Tourism planning (7.4%); • Tourism industry development status and trend (7.0%);	• Tourism resources/ attractions/product development, management and protection (12.11%); • Hotel management (6.62%); • Tourism marketing and market analysis (5.56%);	• Tourism geography (18.9%); • Tourism development of destination and region (16.2%); • Tourism public management and industry management (13.1%); • Tourism planning (7.9%);

- Marketing (4.6%);
- Tourism planning (4.3%);
- Sport (tourism) and leisure (4%);
- Ecotourism (3.7%);
- Tourism education/studies (3.7%);
- Tourism trends (3.3%);
- Community, hosts and guests (2.8%);
- Tourism policy (2.7%);
- Management (2.4%);
- Transport (1.9%);
- Special events (1.5%);
- Human resources (0.8%);
- Business tourism (0.9%);
- Hospitality (0.4%);
- Environmental interpretation (0.1%).

- Ecotourism and sustainable development (7.0%);
- Tourism marketing and market analysis (6.2%);
- Hotel business environment and management (6.2%);
- Basic concepts and theoretical issues in tourism and hospitality (6.0%).

- Tourist behaviour (4.96%);
- MICE (4.63%);
- Tourism economics (3.77%);
- Destination management (3.71%);
- Regional tourism cooperation and development (3.64%);
- Human resources management (3.11%);
- Tourism planning (2.91%);
- Ecotourism (2.78%);
- Other (46.19%) .

- Tourism humanities (6.6%);
- Tourism marketing (6.5%);
- Tourism environment (6.1%);
- Tourism economics (5.5%);
- Tourism theory and research (4.8%);
- Tourism psychology (3.6%);
- Tourism education (3.2%);
- Tourism informationization and application (2.1%);
- Tourism law (1.2%);
- Road and transportation (0.6%);
- Other (3.8%).

Notes: *BISU is the Beijing International Studies University. Figures in parentheses are percentage of the articles on the theme over total articles.

destination and region, tourism public management and industry management, and tourism planning are the significant research themes or disciplinary fields for tourism research (Table 1.1).

Research Methods and Methodologies

There seem to have been rapid changes over the past decade regarding how tourism researchers apply different research methods and methodologies. Huang and Hsu (2008) reviewed 500 articles published in *Tourism Tribune* from 2000 to 2005. They found that 82.6% of the published articles did not clearly state any research methods; these articles resembled the format of an essay or opinion piece more than that of a research paper. Among the reviewed articles, 15% of them applied quantitative methods; the questionnaire survey (9.4%) was found to be the most frequently used quantitative data collection method. Based on the review results, Huang and Hsu (2008) suggest that tourism researchers in China should improve their research training in methods and methodology. A later study by Hsu *et al.* (2010) identified that the percentage of tourism studies applying quantitative methods increased over the years. There is a clear trend that positivism and post-positivism are increasingly adopted by tourism researchers in China, especially among the younger researchers (Hsu *et al.*, 2010). However, in comparison to their international counterparts, very few tourism researchers in China adopted alternative research paradigms, such as interpretivism, constructionism and the critical theory approach (Tribe, 2001).

Outline of this Book

Despite the huge number of articles published in English journals in relation to China tourism (Shen *et al.*, 2014; Zhong *et al.*, 2013), and a few research books dedicated to China tourism (e.g. Lew *et al.*, 2003; Ryan & Gu, 2009; Ryan & Huang, 2013b; Zhang *et al.*, 2005), the communication between tourism researchers in China and their counterparts in Western countries is still limited (Bao *et al.*, 2014). There is still little understanding and knowledge of tourism research in China by academics outside China (Huang & Hsu, 2008; Tsang & Hsu, 2011). Recently, in their co-edited book on China tourism, Ryan and Huang (2013a) noted:

There is an informational asymmetry or imbalance between tourism researchers in China and their international counterparts who mainly work in the English academic language environment. While tourism researchers in China are becoming more able to access and process English academic literature, a large number of researchers working in the Chinese tourism field in the English academic language environment outside China lack the capacity to access and integrate in their works the Chinese language literature produced by tourism researchers in China. (Ryan & Huang, 2013a: 307)

This type of informational asymmetry, representing a significant knowledge gap, prompts the need for the current book. This book provides a thorough review of the tourism research developments in a few key research areas (e.g. community participation in tourism, rural tourism, and tourist market and behaviour studies) and presents to readers outside China a snapshot view of the current state of tourism research in China.

Following this introductory chapter, Chapter 2 provides some philosophical and epistemological views of tourism held by a small number of researchers in China. It is a common perception that tourism studies lack theoretical foundations of their own. However, notably in China, there are some scholars who have developed an understanding of tourism from a theoretical or philosophical point of view. For example, Xie Yanjun, a professor from Dongbei University of Finance and Economics, has published a book talking about foundational theoretical issues in tourism. He has also published journal articles about tourists' experiences, applying a dichotomy of 'tourist world' and 'life world' following the Husserlian phenomenology. Another scholar, Zhang Lingyun, also frequently publishes conceptual articles talking about the essence of tourism. These scholars' work seems to complement the English academic literature in terms of the major theories in tourism (e.g. tourist gaze, tourist destination life cycle model, authenticity) and should be made accessible to a broad audience. A systemic review of these authors' epistemological views of tourism in comparison with some epistemological understandings of tourism in the international (English-speaking) tourism research community can be found in Chapter 2.

Chapter 3 reviews the rural tourism literature in China. There is a rich literature on rural tourism in Chinese journals. Although China is getting more urbanised, most of the tourism resources and attractions are located in rural areas. The rural tourism literature in the Chinese language deals with the multiple facets of the rural economy in China and rural societal realities. Exploring this literature will greatly facilitate our general understanding of tourism in China. A variety of research themes and topics in rural tourism are identified and discussed.

Chapter 4 specifically focuses on community participation and involvement in tourism. Tourism researchers in China have examined and summarised different models of community involvement in tourism development, mostly within an ethnic/rural tourism context. A good number of cases have been presented in published articles. These studies are reviewed, categorised and presented in Chapter 4 as a knowledge area to understand China tourism.

In Chapter 5 we review studies on tourist markets and behaviours in the Chinese literature. Indeed, the Chinese tourism research community has paid more attention to tourism supply issues than to the demand-side issues. Compared to what is available in the tourism literature in English, demand-side tourism research in China is still under-developed. In this chapter, we also apply Lynch *et al.*'s (2012) framework to evaluate the knowledge contribution of tourist markets and behaviour studies in China.

China has a unique and complicated system when it comes to managing tourism resources and attractions. A lot of issues have been discussed and debated in a heated way with regard to tourist attraction management in China. In most cases, as natural resources (e.g. mountain- and water-based) tourist attractions are state owned and thus remain as state assets, local (provincial and sub-provincial) governments are heavily involved in the management of these attractions. The management of these attractions is also influenced by China's general reform roadmap on state-owned enterprises, government system reorganisation and fiscal reform. The issues of tourism attraction management in China are examined in Chapter 6.

Tour guiding is generally under-researched in the international tourism research community. In China, industry practices and problems in relation to tour guiding have been examined by researchers; the China-specific context can offer understanding of tour guiding in a general sense. Researchers in China have also attempted to construct more effective tourist attraction interpretation systems. These attempts and the various studies on tour guiding and tour guide management issues are reviewed and discussed in Chapter 7.

The references given in this book are mainly drawn from four leading Chinese tourism journals from 2006 to 2013. They are *Tourism Tribune*, *Tourism Science*, *Economic Geography* and *Human Geography*. There are other journals that publish tourism research in China (e.g. *Tourism Forum* [formerly the *Journal of Guilin Institute of Tourism*], and the *Journal of Beijing International Studies University*). However, the above-mentioned four journals are well regarded in the tourism research community in China and research articles published in these journals can be used as more credible references to present the overall picture of tourism research in a specific topic area. In some chapters (e.g. Chapters 3 and 4), many case studies are referred to with specific names of places (provinces, counties, townships, villages). For readers' convenience, we have produced a map of China, noting the locations of major case studies included in this book (see Figure 1.1). In addition, we have provided a short compendium of the major tourism reference sources in China in the Appendix to this book.

Figure 1.1 Locations of major case study sites in the book
Key: (1) Beihai Silver Beach National Tourist Resort, Guangxi Province (Guangxi Zhuang Autonomous Region); (2) Dai Garden, Yunnan Province; (3) Diaolou villages, Guangdong Province; (4) Hangzhou Zhijiang National Tourist Resort, Zhejiang Province; (5) Hexigten National Geological Park, Inner Mongolia Autonomous Region; (6) Hongcun village, Anhui Province; (7) Hongkeng village, Fujian Province; (8) Hongsha village, Sichuan Province; (9) Jiuzhaigou National Nature Reserve, Sichuan Province; (10) Langde village, Guizhou Province; (11) Xianhuashan village, Zhejiang Province; (12) Pingan village, Guangxi Province; (13) Wulingyuan National Historic and Scenic Area, Hunan Province; (14) Wuyishan, a World Cultural and Natural Heritage Site, Fujian Province; (15) Xidi village, Anhui Province; (16) Yalong Bay National Tourist Resort, Hainan Province; (17) Yellow Mountain, Anhui Province; (18) Yubeng village, Yunnan Province.
Source: Drawn by the authors.

References

Bao, J. (2009) From idealism to realism to rational idealism: Reflection on 30 years of development in tourism geography in China. *Acta Geographica Sinica* 64 (10), 1184–1102.

Bao, J., Chen, G. and Ma, L. (2014) Tourism research in China: Insights from insiders. *Annals of Tourism Research* 45, 167–181.

Chen, G. and Bao, J. (2011) Progress on overseas studies on China's tourism: A review from the perspective of academic contributions. *Tourism Tribune* 26 (2), 28–35.

China Tourism Education Association (2012) *Annual Report of Tourism Education in China 2012*. Beijing: Tourism Education Press.

CNTA (China National Tourism Administration) (2014) *2013 National Tourism Education and Training Statistics*. See http://www.cnta.gov.cn/html/2014-11/2014-11-6-16-31-28494.html (accessed 19 January 2015).

Hsu, C.H.C., Huang, J. and Huang, S. (2010) Tourism and hospitality research in Mainland China: Trends from 2000 to 2008. In D. Pearce and R. Butler (eds) *Tourism Research: A 20:20 Vision* (pp. 147–160). Oxford: Goodfellow Publishers.

Hu, R. and Huang, S. (2011) A review of doctoral thesis research in tourism management in China. *Journal of Hospitality, Leisure, Sport & Tourism Education* 10 (2), 121–125.

Huang, S. (2001) Problems and solutions on tourism higher education development in China. *Journal of Guilin Institute of Tourism* 12 (2), 66–69.

Huang, S. (2012) Similar exercises, different consequences: An examination of tourism research in national research assessment frameworks. *Tourism Management Perspectives* 2–3, 13–18.

Huang, S. and Hsu, C.H.C. (2008) Recent tourism and hospitality research in China. *International Journal of Hospitality & Tourism Administration* 9 (3), 267–287.

Lew, A.A., Yu, L., Ap, J. and Zhang, G. (eds) (2003) *Tourism in China*. New York: Haworth Hospitality Press.

Lynch, J.G. Jr., Alba, J.W., Krishna, A., Morwitz, V.G. and Gürhan-Canli, Z. (2012) Knowledge creation in consumer research: Multiple routes, multiple criteria. *Journal of Consumer Psychology* 22, 473–485.

Pearce, P. (2011) Career souvenirs. In P. Pearce (ed.) *The Study of Tourism: Foundations from Psychology* (pp. 133–154). Bingley: Emerald.

Pizam, A. (2011) This I believe. In P. Pearce (ed.) *The Study of Tourism: Foundations from Psychology* (pp. 63–78). Bingley: Emerald.

Ryan, C. and Gu, H. (eds) (2009) *Tourism in China: Destination, Cultures and Communities*. New York: Routledge.

Ryan, C. and Huang, S. (2013a) Chinese tourism research: An international perspective. In C. Ryan and S. Huang (eds) *Tourism in China: Destinations, Planning and Experiences* (pp. 304–315). Bristol: Channel View Publications.

Ryan, C. and Huang, S. (2013b) *Tourism in China: Destinations, Planning and Experiences*. Bristol: Channel View Publications.

Shen, Y., Morrison, A.M., Wu, B., Park, J., Li, C. and Li, M. (2014) Where in the world? A geographic analysis of a decade of research in tourism, hospitality, and leisure journals. *Journal of Hospitality & Tourism Research*; doi:10.1177/1096348014563394.

Tribe, J. (2001) Research paradigms and the tourism curriculum. *Journal of Travel Research* 39, 442–448.

Tsang, N.K.F. and Hsu, C.H.C. (2011) Thirty years of research on tourism and hospitality management in China: A review and analysis of journal publications. *International Journal of Hospitality Management* 30 (4), 886–896.

Wu, B., Song, Z. and Deng, L. (2001) A summary of China's tourism research work in the past fourteen years – Academic trends as reflected in 'Tourism Tribune'. *Tourism Tribune* 16 (1), 17–21.

Zhang, G. (2003) Tourism research in China. In A.A. Lew, L. Yu, J. Ap and G. Zhang (eds) *Tourism in China* (pp. 67–82). New York: Haworth Hospitality Press.

Zhang, H.Q., Pine, R. and Lam, T. (2005) *Tourism and Hotel Development in China: From Political to Economic Success*. New York: Haworth Hospitality Press.

Zhang, L., Lan, C., Qi, F. and Wu, P. (2013) Development pattern, classification and evaluation of the tourism academic community in China in the last ten years: From the perspective of big data of articles of tourism academic journals. *Tourism Tribune* 28 (10), 114–125.

Zhong, L., Wu, B. and Morrison, A.M. (2013) Research on China's tourism: A 35-year review and authorship analysis. *International Journal of Tourism Research*; doi:10.1002/jtr.1962.

Zhu, F., Xiang, Y. and Wang, C. (2011) Phenomenon of 'de-tourism' in tourism research and our train of thoughts – based on the analysis of tourism projects sponsored by NSFC and NSSFC. *Tourism Tribune* 26 (11), 28–34.

2 Philosophical and Epistemological Views of Tourism

Introduction

Tourism academics in China may have a way of thinking which is different from those in Western higher learning institutions (Huang *et al.*, 2014; Ryan & Huang, 2013). Such a nuance, while not necessarily and easily observed by tourism academics inside China, is nonetheless important as a starting line of enquiry to investigate how Chinese tourism scholars view tourism epistemologically and how their views differ from their counterparts outside China. A brief review of dominant ideologies and philosophies that have exerted influences on Chinese scholarly thinking may be especially helpful. Confucianism, together with Daoism and Buddhism, were the most influential philosophical schools that guided Chinese intellectual practices until 1911, when the late Qing Dynasty was overthrown by Dr Sun Yat-sen's revolution. From 1911 to 1949, China experienced one of the most turbulent times in its recent history, characterised by the war against Japan's invasion and later the civil war between the communists and the nationalists (Kuomintang). On the intellectual front, the May Fourth Movement led by some public intellectual leaders such as Hu Shih and Chen Duxiu was epoch marking. The May Fourth Movement started serious critical reflections on Confucianism and the Confucian values and embraced some Western thoughts, ideologies and values such as *democracy* and *science*. To some extent, the May Fourth Movement redirected China's intellectual thinking. Many public intellectuals started to critique Confucianism and seek enlightenment from the West. Marxism was introduced to China and later was adopted as a doctrine by the Chinese Communist Party, which became the ruling party of China in 1949.

The cultural and political ideology transitions after 1949 in China were no less dramatic than those before. Egri and Ralston (2004) see three distinctive eras marking social value changes: (1) the Consolidation Era (1950–1965), in which the Chinese Communist Party tried to replace Confucianism with Marxist-Leninist and Maoist ideology; (2) the Era of Cultural Revolution (1966–1976) in which both Confucianism and any Western influences were denounced and censured in order to seek Communist ideological purity; and (3) the Social Reform Era (after 1978) in which Deng Xiaoping's pragmatism, and lately a hybrid of materialism, individualism, liberalism, consumerism, and capitalism, emerged and evolved.

Despite the amorphous and fast-changing nature of cultural influences on a common citizen in modern Chinese society, the academic community in China may still, more or less, be guided by a worldview collectively informed by Confucianism, Marxism and some Western thought. The fundamental differences between the Chinese and Western way of thinking, or cultural mindset, have been contemplated by some scholars. Early in the last century, Lin Yutang, a Chinese scholar who wrote popular essays on Chinese culture in English, argued that there is an entrenched difference between the Western and Chinese ways of thinking (Lin, 1936). According to Lin, while a Western mind is generally analytical and thus science-oriented, there is 'lack of science' in a Chinese mind (Lin, 1936: 80). The Chinese way of thinking is largely intuitive, dialectic or synthetic, non-conclusive and common sense based, while on the contrary, the Western way of thinking is analytical, rational, logically reasoning and truth-seeking. Lin's contemporary, Liang Shumin, also compared the epistemological traditions between China and the West. He noted that, while the Western way of examining the world is static, scientific, mathematical and divisible, the Eastern way of understanding the world, as reflected in traditional Chinese medicine and medical treatment as well as Chinese martial arts, is dynamic, metaphoric, holistic and non-divisible (Liang, 2010).

Tourism, as a formal disciplinary research field in higher learning institutes in China, only appeared after China's opening up to the world in the 1980s. The Chinese institutions, especially in their ideological aspects, do seem to have influenced the way Chinese academics conduct their research in tourism. Understandably, tourism researchers who received their formal education in the socialist system after the foundation of the People's Republic of China in 1949 will likely have been indoctrinated with the Marxist worldview and ideological values (Ryan & Huang, 2013). As remarked by Huang and Hsu (2008), tourism researchers in China tend to resort to dialectic thinking in writing research papers. This indicates that the influences of Marxist dialectical materialism still prevail in Chinese academics' ways of thinking and research writing.

Holding the assumption that Chinese academics may be following a different way of thinking or epistemological approach in conducting tourism research, it is a legitimate and worthy academic concern to see how Chinese academics understand tourism and its associated concepts epistemologically and whether there are differences that could be attributed to the East–West philosophical divide. This chapter provides an attempt to probe such an issue.

Understanding Tourism: Perspectives from the International Academy

In the English-speaking and publishing international tourism academy, defining tourism and constructing frameworks to understand tourism have been at the core of all academic endeavours. Defining tourism seems to be a never-settled research problem. The answer to what tourism is has its many versions. As Smith states:

> What is tourism? The field does not lack answers to this question. In fact, it sometimes appears to have too many answers. Tourism researchers, governmental agencies, tourism associations, and individual businesses have offered different definitions reflecting their own perceptions and interests. (Smith, 1988: 179–180)

As a knowledge field that could fit well into a modern higher education system, tourism was conceived by Jafari and Ritchie (1981) as a study area involving input from many traditional disciplines. Such disciplines include education, sociology, anthropology, psychology, economics, geography, ecology, marketing, business and law. Jafari and Ritchie's (1981) framework of tourism studies involved a total of 16 disciplines and represented a highly analytical one. The framework was useful for informing tourism programmes in universities. However, such a framework suggests a multi-disciplinary view of tourism and it split the understanding of tourism into disciplinary fields that each see tourism as a relevant part of their studies. As a consequence, researchers would hold to their disciplinary boundary lines when studying tourism. And this is the case in early tourism studies. Under such a framework lies the scientific, analytical and positivism tradition of the English-speaking Western learning institutions. Furthermore, there was also an associated constraint derived by disciplinarity. As argued by Sayer (1999), disciplines are parochial and also often imperialist. Early studies of tourism were mostly undertaken by researchers with distinct disciplinary backgrounds; as such, multiple disciplinary perspectives were subconsciously held in understanding (defining) tourism and a common understanding of tourism did not emerge easily in the early days.

Taking a multidisciplinary/interdisciplinary perspective and a systematic approach, Leiper (1979, 1995) views tourism as a system containing the tourists as the human element, geographic elements which include tourist-generating regions, tourist destinations and the transit region/route, resources, and the industrial elements. Leiper's (1979, 1995) systems framework acknowledges tourism as a complex system and includes many phenomenological objects (e.g. people, geographical and industrial components) in the system to make it comprehensive and inclusive. The framework indeed offers a good understanding of the ontological world of tourism and one may argue that it is one of the existing theories that serves the foundations for good tourism planning and governance practices. However, as the framework leans too far toward the phenomenological world, the essence of tourism is not supplied or even implied in any epistemological sense.

If tourism concerns people's life states and their human interactions with places that can be considered tourism-generating regions and destinations, as postulated by Leiper (1979, 1995) and the theorisers in early tourism studies, certainly philosophy does not seem to be an irrelevant discipline or methodology for understanding tourism. Regrettably, philosophy has only been utilised to a very limited degree in the understanding of tourism. Both Jafari and Ritchie's (1981) and Leiper's (1979, 1995) frameworks, as well as their inclinations, do not seem to involve philosophy much in their investigations of tourism. This may be, at least partly, due to the dominating scientism of the tourism academy.

Indeed, as Bertrand Russell (2004) stated, philosophy is something intermediate between theology and science. Philosophy resembles theology in that it consists of speculations on matters about which no definite knowledge has been ascertained; and, like science, it appeals to human reason rather than to authority. To Russell, all *definite* knowledge belongs to science. The divide between philosophy and science as seen by Russell may well explain why philosophy or philosophical thinking has not been widely applied in tourism enquiries.

Despite the seemingly small connection between philosophy and tourism in the academy, some tourism scholars did see that philosophy could contribute to the epistemology of tourism. This has been illuminated both in published journal articles and in book volumes (e.g. Tribe, 1997, 2006,

2009). In his attempt to dismiss the argument that tourism can be a discipline in the traditional sense, Tribe (1997) included philosophy in parallel with other disciplines like sociology and economics as a discipline that contributes to the creation of tourism knowledge. He views the body of tourism knowledge as not only created by one or more disciplines interfacing with the field of tourism, but also by the knowledge practices by multiple parties, including industry, government, think-tanks, interest groups, research institutes and consultancies in the phenomenal world. The latter is mostly enabled outside any disciplinary framework, and thus can be characterised as 'extradisciplinary' in comparison with the former as 'multidisciplinary'. The majority of such knowledge production as located within the external world occurs within the business spheres; due to the *postmodern condition* and/ or performativity as elaborated by Lyotard (1984), business-related tourism knowledge production has overpowered non-business related tourism knowledge production.

In his effort to further theorise tourism knowledge creation, Tribe (2006) borrowed the theory of force-fields (Lewin, 1935) in illustrating the mechanism of tourism knowledge generation. He contends that the interplay and interactions of the five knowledge force-field factors (namely *person, rules, position, ends* and *ideology*) mediates the phenomenal world of tourism and its corresponding knowledge world. As the result of mediation of the knowledge force-field factors and their interactions, the revealed knowledge world of tourism cannot truthfully reflect the phenomenal world of tourism. To the authors of this book, Tribe's (2006) knowledge force-field framework has so far been the most useful theory to understand the relationship between the ontology and epistemology of tourism. The framework also represents an outcome of systemic philosophical reasoning which is commonly practised in tourism academia.

Tribe's (2006) theory highlights the double selectivity that operates in the construction of tourism knowledge. On the one hand, selectivity happens when the researcher casts a gaze into the world of tourism. The researcher is susceptible to the actions and the influences of the other knowledge force-field factors (e.g. rules, ends, ideology). On the other hand, the processing of the research is also directly influenced by the knowledge force-field, which may come completely out of the researcher's volitional control. The researcher and her/his situatedness inevitably exerted the influence on what stories are told and how they are told.

The knowledge force-field framework can better guide our understanding of tourism research across cultural and paradigm borders. In China, tourism research is undertaken in a different knowledge force-field environment from that of most Western countries. While the trend of cultural convergence is obvious due to China's further integration into the world, all the five factors, *person, rules, position, ends* and *ideology*, if scrutinised closely, would exhibit different, if not contrasting, aspects and characteristics in China compared to what is understood in English-speaking academia. Therefore, it would be illuminating to see how academics in China construct their understanding and knowledge of tourism. The following sections provide a systemic review of the Chinese indigenous scholar's epistemological pursuit of tourism.

The Meanings of 'Travel' and 'Tourism': Linguistic and Cultural Differences

Before examining the views and perspectives of Chinese academics in understanding tourism, it is necessary to note the literal differences of travel and tourism between the Western and Chinese languages. Language is the most representational feature of a culture and people's interpretation and construction of meanings of the same phenomenon could be constrained and limited by the language they are using. The Chinese language, especially in its written forms, is as old as Chinese civilisation can continuously be traced back. Words in different languages always carry cultural and ethnic connotations. In China, as the same Chinese character could have been used for millennia, its modern use and associated meaning also take on layers of meaning as it evolves historically.

In the Western context, the word 'travel' refers to people movement. The English word 'travel' came from French word 'travail', with an original connotation of toil and hardship en route. Nevertheless, travelling in olden times was full of hardship, danger and difficulties (Zhang, 2006). However, in English culture, travel may also take on other endowed cultural meaning and humanity values. Francis Bacon (1561–1626), in his essay *Of Travel*, elaborates:

TRAVEL, in the younger sort, is a part of education, in the elder, a part of experience. He that travelleth into a country, before he hath some entrance into the language, goeth to school, and not to travel. That young men travel under some tutor, or grave servant, I allow well; so that he be such a one that hath the language, and hath been in the country before; whereby he may be able to tell them what things are worthy to be seen, in the country where they go; what acquaintances they are to seek; what exercises, or discipline, the place yieldeth. For else, young men shall go hooded, and look abroad little. It is a strange thing, that in sea voyages, where there is nothing to be seen, but sky and sea, men should make diaries; but in land-travel, wherein so much is to be observed, for the most part they omit it; as if chance were fitter to be registered, than observation. Let diaries, therefore, be brought in use. (Bacon, n.d.)

Bacon's view of travel may represent one of the sociocultural expectations of his time that led to the prevalence of the Grand Tour. From a linguistic and cultural perspective, this may lead to the associated connotation of travel as a privilege occupied by the upper social class, wealthy and well-educated aristocracy. On the contrary, the word 'tourism' had its root in Latin ('tounare') and Greek ('tornos') with an original meaning of circled movement around a central point or axis (Theobald, 2005). Tourism, as a modern English word, suggests the action of movement around a circle in a linguistic sense. In the Western cultural context, unlike the meaning which is fixed to 'travellers' from the Grand Tour era, the word 'tourists' carries much more of a negative image and cultural contempt due to post-industrial mass tourism development in the developed world. Tourists are typically stereotyped as people who travel en masse, bargain for cheap goods, flaunt their spending and are ignorant of culture (Theobald, 2005). Therefore, it is not unusual to see people from Western cultures identifying themselves as travellers rather than tourists.

In the language environment of mainland China, the most commonly conceived words for 'travel' is *'lvxing'* ('旅行') while that for 'tourism' is *'lvyou'* ('旅游'). The Chinese character *'旅'* (*'lv'*) generally carries a meaning equivalent to 'travel'. The word *'行'* in Chinese literally means 'walk'. Comparatively, while *'旅行'* can be regarded as capturing most of the meaning of the English word 'travel', the Chinese words *'旅游'* deviates in its meaning from the English word 'tourism' more pronouncedly. Wang (2014) argues that, in contrast to the Indo-European languages, Chinese characters represent a picture-based style of thinking. The Chinese words *'旅游'* can be understood as travelling for the purpose of *'游'*; while the word *'游'* can be hardly regarded as taking the meaning of 'tourism' in English.

As a matter of fact, the Chinese word *'游'* has been used for over 3000 years. The word takes its original pictorial meaning as a 'flag flowing in the wind', which is further derived as human play and gaming with uncompromised freedom (Cao, 2013). In Chinese, the word *'游'* has been used together with other Chinese words to form many different two-word phrases, with a subject's state of freedom for one's body, soul and spirit as defined by the word *'游'*. This state of being can be best illustrated by Chuang Tsu, the defining figure along with Lao Tsu in Chinese Taoism. In his work *Free and Easy Wandering* (逍遥游) (note here the word '游' is in the Chinese title), he wrote:

> In the northern darkness there is a fish and his name is K'un. The K'un is so huge I don't know how many thousand li he measures. He changes and becomes a bird whose name is P'eng. The back of the P'eng measures I don't know how many thousand li across and, when he rises up and flies off, his wings are like clouds all over the sky. When the sea begins to move, this bird sets off for the southern darkness, which is the Lake of Heaven. (trans. B. Watson)

The state of *you* '游' thus represents a state of being that can be transformative and can help an individual to achieve complete internal freedom. And in the *Book of Songs*, the word '游' was used to denote activities not only by the aristocracy, but also by grass-roots people (Wang, 2014). Therefore, from an ethnolinguistic perspective, 'tourism' in Chinese takes a different etymological meaning from what is understood in the Western context. Such nuanced etymological differences should be taken into consideration when examining Chinese scholars' academic pursuit of defining tourism epistemologically.

The Essence of Tourism: Chinese Perspectives

As is the case in the English-speaking tourism research academy, in China only a small number of tourism scholars have chosen to study the essence of tourism from an epistemological perspective. This section is not intended to provide the most comprehensive review of the views of those scholars who have made such academic attempts in China; rather, it is to introduce influential views from some established scholars.

Tourism world versus life world

Tourism is a complex social and economic phenomenon, in which the core element is the tourist (tourism) experience. Xie Yanjun, a professor from Dongbei University of Finance and Economics, started his enquiry into the essence of tourism from the perspective of phenomenology. He and his colleague (Xie & Xie, 2006) submitted the concept 'tourism world' versus 'life world' to construct an epistemology of tourism. To Xie, despite the different purposes of individual tourists, they all go to a different place and return after spending some time there; they not only spend money when taking part in tourism, but more importantly they spend whole blocks of time. In a sense, the time tourists spend is different in nature from time spent in their working/living environs. It is mostly leisure time! However, the activities in which tourists engage during tourism and their meanings differ greatly from those in their daily living environment.

To understand tourism, it is necessary to differentiate tourism as a phenomenon or a set of phenomena from daily (home) life phenomena, so that the essential characters of tourism and the tourism experience can be disclosed (Xie & Xie, 2006). Xie and Xie (2006) base their construction of tourism on the two terms: *tourism world* and *life world*. *Life world* is the world in which a person lives on a daily basis; it consists of all the events relevant to his daily life, but excludes events in the tourism world. The assumption here is that tourism is a process of experience which is different from daily life experience. In the daily *life world*, the experiences of an individual are constructed around life events like work, study and daily living, and some occasional happenings such as seeing a doctor or attending a children's birthday party. The summation of these events will influence people's emotional states, generating feelings like boredom, dislike, shame, frustration and sadness. And to a large extent, these emotional states construct the driving force of tourism (Xie & Xie, 2006). It seems that Xie and Xie's (2006) description of these negating human feelings is no different from the state conceptualised by Graham Dann (1977) as 'anomie'. Dann (1977) treats anomie as a push travel motivation. Anomie represents the desire to transcend the feeling of isolation obtained in everyday life; people simply wish to 'get away from it all'.

Unlike the everyday life world, the tourism world represents a brand new life sphere. It contrasts with the life world in two dimensions. In the spatial dimension, tourism is a form of temporary severance from the life world, first leaving it and then returning to it. In this process of departing and regressing, tourists experience a series of changes. In the time dimension, the time the tourist spends in the place different from his living place will be permanent 'leaking-out' or 'leakage' to the integral time the person owns in the (daily) life world. If the totality of the person's life is only defined by his life world, such leakage of time would be in the real sense. However, in reality, the person also seeks meaning from the tourism world, thus making the amount of time leaked out of the life world meaningful to the self and full of discoveries. Such type of self-proof and discovery is realised through tourism as a process of experience. Tourism experience, therefore, is a psychological process as well as a physical process, a temporal phenomenon as well as a spatial phenomenon, an individual behaviour as well as a social behaviour. Based on these arguments,

Xie and Xie (2006) regard the process of tourism experience as a self-organising continuing system. It is composed of a series of unique and meaningful scenarios and events.

Juxtaposing the tourism world with the life world would enable a full understanding of tourism. On the one hand, tourism is an extension of people's life world; on the other, tourism constructs a world which is completely different from the life world. It is a complete system with a unique structure. From the phenomenological perspective, tourism represents phenomena occurring in a special world, and these phenomena are different from daily life phenomena.

In constructing their tourism epistemology, Xie and Xie (2006) went further in identifying the basic elements and contents of the tourism world. They are as follows:

- the tourism tempo-spatial relations;
- the system of tourist attractions;
- tourists;
- the interactions between the tourist and other people;
- the intermediate elements that support the occurrence of tourism; and
- signals and signalling elements that form and communicate tourism meanings.

The underpinning theory of Xie and Xie's (2006) tourism epistemology is Husserl phenomenology. Husserl's concept of 'lebenswelt', or 'life world', is one of the foundational concepts of Husserl phenomenology. However, the Husserl *life world* is not equivalent to the daily life world; it is a lively world of experience. The Husserl *life world* is a purposeless structure, a phenomenological state of existence, so much so that it is distinguished from daily life which is driven by varied purposes. The Husserl life world is thus not the sense of a world from the natural science and cosmological perspective. It is the world as experienced by a life subject through his specific perspective; however, it may be distorted. Xie and Xie (2006) modified the scope of the Husserl life world and referred their own concept of life world as daily life world in comparison to tourism world. From a tourism perspective, the phenomenological life world can be regarded as a tempo-spatial continuum composed of both daily life world and tourism world. Hereby the daily life world is what is meant by Xie and Xie (2006) in their tourism epistemology as the life world, a counterpart concept to mirror the tourism world.

From a phenomenological perspective, the typology of *tourism world* and *life world* advances the philosophical thinking about tourism among Chinese scholars. Long and Lu (2010) borrowed Xie and Xie's (2006) concepts of tourism world and life world to further establish an explanatory framework of tourism experience. Also holding the Husserl philosophical perspective, Long and Lu argue that the tourism world is not determined by its physicality, but by the transposition of the subjective perspective. It is because tourists take a different perspective to gaze into others' *life world* that *tourism world* can be formed. Such a perspective transposition is in essence due to the transposition of mind, which enables tourists (people) to enter into a different life state and lifestyle. The tourism world provides spaces and conditions for such a mind transposition, thereby gaining them status in an unusual life sphere. Therefore, what defines the tourism world is not its physical constituents, but the tourist's subjective mind state. And it is such a *mind state* that makes the tourism world exhibit characteristics like emotion orientation, self-regressing and self-purporting (i.e. finding purpose within the activities itself), which are different from that of the life world.

Deploying the phenomenological method, Xie (2010) went further in the quest for the essence of tourism. He explicitly stated that Husserl's method of *suspending* and *bracketing away* would be useful to probe the essence of tourism. Husserl's phenomenological reduction is a suitable method to study the essence of tourism. Xie argues that in the process of reducing experiential facts to essential generalities, the essence of tourism can only be revealed by looking into tourist experiences, rather than any external impact of tourism phenomena. Using Husserl's *suspending* method and a small indicative student sample, Xie (2010) submitted that tourism is a leisure experience people gain by using their recreation time in a different place. According to Xie (2010), three commonalities that can define tourism are: experience (aesthetic impression and pleasurable feelings); different place (being away from the residential place); and recreational time (time not used for work or study).

Defining tourism: Views and debates

Like Xie, other scholars in China have attempted to define tourism epistemologically. Academic debates about the different views and definitions are not unusual. Zhang Lingyun's quest for the essence of tourism started with a review of the definitions of tourism in the international tourism academia. He reviewed a total of 30 different definitions as documented in tourism textbooks, government reports, World Tourism Organisation official documents, reports from industry associations and international tourism academic organisations (Zhang, 2008a). Through critically reviewing these tourism definitions, Zhang (2008a) summarised the essential characteristics as follows:

- Tourism represents people's spatial movement, and such movement is temporary.
- Tourism can be carried out with one or more motivations.
- Tourism activities need certain transport facilities, accommodation, marketing systems, recreation and attraction services as the supporting system. These form the base of the tourism industry.
- Tourism is not only tourists' personal leisure and recreational consumption. Spatially, tourism involves not only unidirectional people flow from the source market to the destination; it is a complete spatial system connecting the tourist source region, the transit routes and the destination.
- The tourism spatial system is not only an economic system, but also more importantly a cultural and social system.

Zhang (2008a) also appreciates the Husserl phenomenological *reduction/ suspending* method as the right approach to seek the essence of tourism and proposes that a philosophical elucidation be taken in order to understand the essence of tourism. He thus develops his understanding of tourism at two levels: (1) tourism is a temporary lifestyle and state of living in which people seek a differentiated experience against their usual life and work environment or familiar people–place relations and interpersonal relations; it is a negation of the usual life state and scenarios; (2) tourism is the summation of the social relations and phenomena derived by individuals' innate needs and behaviours (to negate the usual life state and living relations).

In Zhang's journey to seek the essence of tourism, he further developed the concept of 'unusual environment' in construing tourism (Zhang, 2008b). Unusual environment refers to the environment outside people's daily life, study and work and includes both natural and cultural environment. Zhang's view of tourism is thereby built upon two polemics: *unusual environment* as the objective factor of tourism, and *experience* which he sees as the subjective factor. Consequently, Zhang (2008b) views tourism as people's experience and lifestyles towards (in) unusual environment.

Unusual environment (other place) and usual environment (home place) are the two aspects of an antagonistic and unifying contradiction. An understanding of unusual environment can be generated by studying usual environment. Like Dann (1977) and Xie and Xie (2006), Zhang looked into the historical evolution of human society from agricultural to industrial and post-industrial. Industrialisation brings mankind material wealth and at the same time causes the degradation of the ecological environment and the overexploitation of natural resources. As a consequence, human beings are full of contradictions and anxiety over industrialisation and modernisation. They cannot refuse; neither can they have options. Such a state of humanity represents the alienation of humankind and ignites the desire to get away from the alienated usual living place temporarily and go into the past to find the dreamed 'homeland'. Although unusual environment attracts tourists, few tourists would like to transform unusual environment into usual environment. It is the usual environment that provides an individual with substance and support and enables him to make a living.

Zhang (2008b) argues that tourism as experience in an unusual environment is imbued with non-normal behaviours. Compared to usual environment experiences, unusual environment experiences are a temporary avoidance and negation of the daily life. Zhang assumes that the desire to experience unusual environment is prenatal, innate and associated with human imagination and rebellion, irrespective of the levels of social economic development.

In another paper, Zhang (2009) further focused on the concept of unusual environment and attempted to construct his version of tourism epistemology. He elaborated that usual environment and unusual environment in combination define a subject's phenomenological world. In this sense, Zhang's (2009) model does not seem to significantly differ from Xie and Xie's (2006) framework of *tourism world* versus *life world*. Drawing on typical experiences of modern living, Zhang notes that usual environment can be flowing, unfixed and cross-territorial. Some mobile workers, such as tour guides and escorts, take their usual environment with them; while cross-border commuters, such as those commuting between Shenzhen and Hong Kong for living/working, are still in their usual environment and should not be regarded as taking part in tourism. On the other hand, unusual environment can be volitionally selected, is not pre-determined and has no set borders. It constructs a necessary condition for tourism, but not a sufficient condition, as much of unusual environment is not valid to individual tourists if not experienced by them. To individual tourists, unusual environment is not only a geographic concept, but also a psychological concept. Therefore, unusual environment is a multidimensional living space and psychological/behavioural environment. In this environment, human behaviour is a function of both human and environmental factors.

It should be noted that both Xie Yanjun (Xie, 2010) and Zhang Lingyun (Zhang, 2008b, 2009) attempted to construct a tourism 'discipline' in their quests for the essence of tourism. It appears naturally that both authors are partly motivated by an intellectual conscience to construct the tourism discipline, as they both work as academics in Chinese universities where tourism is not treated as a well-established discipline. As stated by Xie, his paper 'starts from the perspective of constructing a tourism knowledge commonwealth (discipline)' (Xie, 2010: 26, authors' translation). Zhang (2009: 12, authors' translation) intended to 'use a brand new perspective, to scrutinise tourism phenomenon and essence, and try to use the concept of unusual environment to reconstruct the disciplinary framework of tourism studies'.

Following Zhang (2008b, 2009), Wang and Zou (2011) build upon the concept of *unusual environment* to examine the meaning of tourist experience. They argue that the essence of experience in unusual environment is to adjust the life state. Humans are motivated to seek new life experiences or adjust the life state. In so doing, they justify the meaning of life and of being human. Wang and Zou quote existentialism and argue that different types of human experiences will enable the meaning of life and justify an individual's existence. Tourism is such a human experience that happens in an unusual environment and enriches the meaning of life. They further argue that tourism is characterised by some human behaviours driven by some human motivations; however, it is the environment in which these behaviours happen that distinguishes these behaviours from others. An unusual environment thus can provide the following to justify human existence and the meaning of life:

- new living elements in new environment;
- severance from and avoidance of old environment;
- stimuli and reference for the meaning of life;
- opportunities for a different life role; and
- reconstruction of self in combination with the environment.

Holding an existentialist view, Wang and Zou (2011) extended Zhang's (2009) definition of tourism on the basis of the concept of *unusual environment*. They added four additional definitional aspects:

(1) Tourism, as human experience in unusual environment, must be actively pursued by the human subject; in such a sense, exiled prisoners, even in an unusual environment, would not be treated as tourists.
(2) Tourism as human experience in an unusual environment is temporary. Tourists have to return to their usual environment to sustain their living substances. No matter how repressive and alienating their usual environment is, tourists have to live with it as it provides the base and resources for their living and existence.

(3) Tourism experience can be substituted for other experiences to meet the same human ends in order to seek life meanings. Tourism is a means to such human ends. In other words, tourism is experience, but not all experience is tourism.

(4) The value of tourism experience is limited. To some people, other ways of searching for a meaningful life seem to be more effective. There have been great thinkers, philosophers, writers and monks throughout history who have understood the meaning of life better than others but who did not travel much.

The academic quest for the essence of tourism has also been embodied in some scholarly debates and dialogues. After Xie and Zhang published their views on the issue, Wang Yuhai, a professor specialising in tourism basic theories and tourism culture in Beijing, provided a critique on both Xie's and Zhang's views of the essence of tourism (Wang, 2010: 12). He acknowledged both scholars' contributions in clarifying the concept of tourism. Wang came up with his own definition of tourism: 'tourism is people's experience in unusual environment using leisure time, and is a temporary life style and life state' (authors' translation). Such a definition does not substantially differ from Zhang's definition.

Wang's definition of tourism was further questioned by Professor Cao Shitu (Cao, 2013), who also published a book in Chinese on tourism philosophy (Cao, 2008). Cao (2013) first questioned the validity of defining tourism as 'people's experience in unusual environment using leisure time', noting that 'experiencing unusual environment' is not the essential purpose of tourism. Furthermore, 'unusual environment' was criticised by Cao (2013) as a complex and confusing concept without clear meaning and scope. Instead, he proposed the use of 'different place' as a simpler alternative. Referring to the ethnolinguistic meaning of the Chinese character '游' as a state of freedom with body and mind, Cao (2013: 116) assumes that the essence of tourism lies in 'the experience that set free body and mind in a different place'. Cao (2013: 116) submits that 'tourism is people's experience with both body and mind freedom through using leisure time to travel to, tour and stay in a place outside their daily life and work environment and for the purposes of recreation, aesthetics, and knowledge-seeking, etc.' (authors' translation). Cao emphasises that tourism is a 'game' activity (human beings' freedom state). The essence of tourism, in a philosophic sense, resides in the Chinese word '游', with the connotation of 'pursuit of freedom'.

Cao and his colleagues seem to take a philosophical lens to define tourism. They argue that, from a philosophic perspective, tourism is 'experience', referring to tourists' state of freedom of body and mind in a different place (Cao *et al.*, 2011). Therefore, experience, rather than anything else, represents the essence of tourism. The reasons are as follows:

- Experience is the most general, pervasive and stable property of tourism phenomena.
- Experience can differentiate tourism effectively from other phenomena: all the defining characteristics (e.g. occurring in other place, being temporary and leisure-based) can be derived from tourism experience.
- Experience is the basic factor that defines and influences the non-essential features in tourism phenomena.
- Experience is the *raison d'être* for the generation, change and development of tourism activities.

The survival theory of tourism phenomenon

As China has been in a socialist ideological system, one may wonder whether Chinese scholars' understanding of tourism might be directed by a Marxist philosophy and worldview. Indeed, some scholars have interpreted tourism using the Marxist historical materialism perspective. Zhang Bin is one of these. Zhang (2008, 2012) holds that tourism can only happen after human beings meet their physical survival needs and life-sustaining needs. Only then can tourism needs and behaviours happen. According to Marxist historical materialism, mankind has to make a living in order to make history. In order to survive, people first of all have to produce living material that meets their biological needs like eating, drinking, sleeping, etc. Therefore, the *first* human historical activity is to produce material life. Taking a sociohistorical perspective, human activities can be classified into three domains: those that meet human biological needs; those meeting the needs to sustain living and produce living material; and those that are beyond the above-mentioned for advanced human needs in areas of politics, science, arts and religion, and thus are called non-life-sustaining activities. Both leisure and tourism belong to the third category of activities. Leisure is a life state in which a human being does not need to consider the basic problem of survival. However, leisure happens in people's daily living environment.

Zhang (2008) sees tourism as distinct from leisure in two aspects: (1) tourism generally requires more accumulation of the material for sustaining life than leisure does; and (2) tourism happens in a different living environment from where leisure occurs. The realisation of tourism means that people leave their usual life environment and enter a different place, other people's life environment. This different place, to the host people there, is familiar, effective, secure, habitual and routine. But to tourists, if they wish to produce life-sustaining material and meet non-life-sustaining needs, such a place, as their unusual environment, appears to be strange, ineffective, insecure, unaccustomed and temporary. They have to resort to their wealth accumulated in their own life-making environment in order to support their activities in such an unusual environment. Therefore, although tourists' activities in the tourism world appear not to be relevant to, or even contradictory to their life-making activities in their daily life world, in essence, tourists are decisively influenced by their usual life environment. Tourism has to end by tourists' return to usual life. On this basis, Zhang (2008) argues that the tourism environment as constructed by the subject, object and the relations in the tourism process, is not a stand-alone world squeezed out of the life world; rather, it is based on the residential place of the usual life environment, and subject to the influence and limitation of the usual life environment.

Guided by the Marxist historical materialism, Zhang (2008) believes that on the basis of human survival theory, the essence of tourism and the associated intrinsic laws can be disclosed, and thus tourism can be defined. To Zhang (2008), tourism refers to human life activities through which people plan, leave and return to their usual life environment to experience and satiate their non-life-sustaining needs.

Conclusion

This chapter provides a comparative review on Chinese indigenous scholars' epistemological understandings of tourism. The chapter sets the stage by briefing on the differences of thinking between the West and China. It notes that the Chinese way of thinking may be directed by some Chinese cultural traditions but nevertheless the recent introduction of Marxism as the orthodox ideology and some Western thoughts would also exert influences on Chinese academics' intellectual work. In the English-speaking tourism academia, attempts at defining tourism are many. Most early articles in this regard seemed to take a positivistic view and position tourism as a field of study in a multidisciplinary framework. Although tourism as a complex human phenomenon would be worthy of philosophical enquiry, for a long time tourism has not been studied sufficiently from a philosophical perspective. Tourism and philosophy are yet to be married in academic enquiries.

Understanding the essence of tourism would naturally prompt an enquirer to probe into philosophical issues. In China, the cultural and linguistic connotations associated with Chinese words for 'tourism' should be taken into consideration when understanding the meaning of tourism. The Chinese word '游' denotes a state of being which frees up one's body, mind and spirit. Such a state of being would be pursued and enjoyed by all social members, irrespective of their social class. Therefore, to Chinese people, tourism may represent a more desired-for life state. Certainly, Chinese people are less concerned about being called 'tourists' than those from Western countries.

This chapter elaborates on a small number of selected scholars' views and scholarly works on the essence of tourism. These include: Professor Xie Yanjun's views and framework of understanding tourism by differentiating the tourism world from the life world; Professor Zhang Lingyun's construction of the 'unusual environment' concept in seeking for the essence of tourism; Professor Cao Shitu's critiques on Xie and Zhang's definitions of tourism and his own seemingly more indigenous interpretation of tourism from the cultural meaning of the Chinese word '游'; and Zhang Bin's view of tourism using Marxist historical materialism as an analytical framework. All these epistemological views of tourism are embodied in scholarly works published in Chinese. However, they seem to be important and influential to further direct tourism research in China and should be made known to the tourism academia outside China.

References

Bacon, F. (n.d.) *Essays of Francis Bacon – Of Travel*. See http: //www.authorama.com/ essays-of-francis-bacon-19.html (accessed 25 September 2014).

Cao, S. (2008) *An Introduction to Tourism Philosophy*. Tianjin: Nankai University Press.

Cao, S. (2013) A further study on the concept of tourism – a discussion with Professor Wang Yu-hai, etc. *Human Geography* 28 (1), 116–120.

Cao, S., Cao, G. and Deng, S. (2011) A philosophical analysis of the essence of tour. *Tourism Science* 25 (1), 80–87.

Chung Tsu. (n.d.) *Free and Easy Wandering* (Trans. B. Watson). See http: //terebess.hu/ english/chuangtzu.html#1.

Dann, G. (1977) Anomie, ego-enhancement and tourism. *Annals of Tourism Research* 4 (4), 184–194.

Egri, C.P. and Ralston, D.A. (2004) Generation cohorts and personal values: A comparison of China and the United States. *Organizational Science* 15 (2), 210–220.

Huang, S. and Hsu, C.H.C. (2008) Recent tourism and hospitality research in China. *International Journal of Hospitality & Tourism Administration* 9 (3), 267–287.

Huang, S., van der Veen, R. and Zhang, G. (2014) Editorial essay: New era of China tourism research. *Journal of China Tourism Research* 10 (4), 379–387.

Jafari, J. and Ritchie, J.R.B. (1981) Toward a framework for tourism education: Problems and prospects. *Annals of Tourism Research* 8 (1), 13–34.

Leiper, N. (1979) The framework of tourism: Towards a definition of tourism, tourist, and the tourist industry. *Annals of Tourism Research* 6 (4), 390–407.

Leiper, N. (1995) *Tourism Management*. Collingwood, Victoria: TAPE Publications.

Lewin, K. (1935) *A Dynamic Theory of Personality*. New York: McGraw-Hill.
Liang, S. (2010) *The Fate of Chinese Culture [中国文化的命运]*. Beijing: China CITIC Press.
Lin, Y. (1936) *My Country and My People*. London: William Heinemann.
Long, J. and Lu, C. (2010) From life-world to tourism-world: Across the state of mind. *Tourism Tribune* 25 (6), 25–31.
Lyotard, J. (1984) *The Postmodern Condition: A Report on Knowledge*. Manchester: Manchester University Press.
Russell, B. (2004) *History of Western Philosophy* (2nd edn). London: Routledge.
Ryan, C. and Huang, S. (2013) Chinese tourism research: An international perspective. In C. Ryan and S. Huang (eds) *Tourism in China: Destinations, Planning and Experiences* (pp. 304–315). Bristol: Channel View Publications.
Sayer, A. (1999) *Long Live Postdisciplinary Studies! Sociology and the Curse of Disciplinary Parochialism/Imperialism*. See http://www.lancaster.ac.uk/fass/sociology/research/publications/papers/sayer-long-live-postdisciplinary-studies.pdf (accessed 19 September 2014).
Smith, S.L.J. (1988) Defining tourism: A supply-side view. *Annals of Tourism Research* 15, 179–190.
Theobald, W.F. (2005) The meaning, scope and measurement of travel and tourism. In W.F. Theobald (ed.) *Global Tourism* (3rd edn) (pp. 5–24). Amsterdam: Elsevier.
Tribe, J. (1997) The indiscipline of tourism. *Annals of Tourism Research* 24 (3), 638–657.
Tribe, J. (2006) The truth about tourism. *Annals of Tourism Research* 33 (2), 360–381.
Tribe, J. (ed.) (2009) *Philosophical Issues in Tourism*. Bristol: Channel View Publications.
Wang, X. and Zou, T. (2011) On the significance of experience under unusual environment. *Tourism Tribune* 26 (7), 19–23.
Wang, Y. (2010) A new exploration of the concept of 'tourism' – discussion with Professor Xie Yanyun and Zhang Lingyun. *Tourism Tribune* 25 (12), 12–17.
Wang, Z. (2014) Language predicament on the definitions of 'tourism' and its breaking through. *Tourism Forum* 7 (2), 16–25.
Xie, Y. (2010) On the essence of tourism and its way of cognition – viewing from the perspective of the discipline itself. *Tourism Tribune* 25 (1), 26–31.
Xie, Y. and Xie, Z. (2006) Tourist experience in the tourist world: A study in the perspective of phenomenology. *Tourism Tribune* 21 (4), 13–18.
Zhang, B. (2008) The essence of tourism phenomena on the premise of the survival theory. *Tourism Science* 22 (6), 10–14.
Zhang, B. (2012) What kind of tourism philosophy do we need? Comment on 'An Introduction to Tourism Philosophy'. *Tourism Tribune* 27 (9), 106–112.
Zhang, L. (2008a) Review on the definitions and concept of tourism currently popular in the world – recognition of the nature of tourism. *Tourism Tribune* 23 (1), 86–91.
Zhang, L. (2008b) A study on consumers' behaviour and phenomenon under unusual environment. *Tourism Tribune* 23 (10), 12–16.
Zhang, L. (2009) Unusual environment: The core concept of tourism research – a new framework for tourism research. *Tourism Tribune* 24 (7), 12–17.
Zhang, Y. (2006) From TRAVEL to TOURISM: On changes of the concept TOURISM in England in the 19th century. *Tourism Science* 20 (2), 1–5.

3 Rural Tourism Development in China

Introduction

China is a country in which a significant number of people live in rural areas. Although at the end of 2011, China's urban population exceeded its rural population for the first time and the country is moving rapidly in its urbanisation (Bloomberg, 2012), in terms of tourism development, especially in domestic tourism, rural cultural and natural landscapes form the basis of China's tourism development. When China develops further, tourist attractions in China's vast rural regions will essentially provide more of the space demanded for tourism activities, and understandably the country's growing number of urban residents will need to release their city-living pressures through tourism. As such, rural tourism facilities will meet people's needs to seek relaxation and enhance personal health and wellbeing (Tan *et al.*, 2010).

Rural tourism is a very broad field of research. In the international research community, a clear definition or definitive framework of rural tourism is still required. Nevertheless, Lane's (1994) definition of rural tourism is well received and widely cited. According to Lane (1994), rural tourism, as a concept, is a form of tourism that is located in rural areas, is rural in scale, character and function, reflecting the differing and complex pattern of the rural environment, economy, history and location (Gao *et al.*, 2009). By the early 1990s, there already existed a significant literature on rural tourism in the English-speaking academic world (Lane, 1994; Sharpley & Roberts, 2004). In comparison, China's rural tourism started in the late 1980s and only gained development momentum from the mid-1990s (Lin & Dai, 2006); research on rural tourism in China seemed to start in the 1990s (Liu & Jiang, 2011) and, since then, a rapidly growing body of Chinese literature on rural tourism has been developed. Despite such a significant body of Chinese literature regarding rural tourism in China, it seems that little is known about China's rural tourism development outside China (Gao *et al.*, 2009). This chapter, therefore, provides a thorough review of the research published in the major Chinese tourism journals regarding rural tourism in China. Consistent with the other chapters, a comparative lens was taken in this review. We first present a brief review of the research themes and issues on rural tourism in the international research community; then we review the Chinese literature on rural tourism. At the end of the chapter, we briefly note and discuss the difference of research foci of rural tourism in and outside China before concluding the chapter.

Research Themes in Rural Tourism: International Perspectives

Worldwide, rural tourism is a phenomenon that has been resorted to in order to counteract the declining primary sector economies in many countries and to help diversify rural economic and social development (Gannon, 1994; Gartner, 2004; Greffe, 1994). The rural environment increasingly provides resources for tourism development while facing diminishing importance in other economic activities (Sharpley & Roberts, 2004). In the English tourism literature, there were two special journal issues dedicated to research into rural tourism internationally – one in the *Journal of Sustainable Tourism (JoST)* in 1994 and another in the *International Journal of Tourism Research (IJTR)* 10 years later in 2004. As noted by Sharpley and Roberts (2004: 123), the special edition of *JoST* in 1994 'identified a great deal of potential for rural tourism as a phenomenon and as an integral part of rural structuring'. Sharpley and Roberts (2004), as guest editors of the *IJTR* special issue, identified that the issues raised in the *JoST* special collection remained valid in 2004 despite some theoretical development and some increasingly documented empirical studies. The common themes of rural tourism research demonstrated in the two special volumes include:

- the role of government in rural tourism;
- social and human resource capacity in rural tourism development;
- stakeholder involvement; and
- knowledge expertise.

Until 2004, most of the above-identified themes and issues seemed to be unanswered or not satisfactorily resolved (Sharpley & Roberts, 2004). In their editorial paper to accompany the 2004 *IJTR* special issue, Sharpley and Roberts (2004) further summarised the state of research in rural tourism in three areas: (a) rurality and rural tourism: definitive and conceptualisation issues; (b) rural tourism as sustainable activity; and (c) rural tourism as an agent of rural development.

Several books can be found specifically on the subject of rural tourism (e.g. Roberts & Hall, 2001; Hall *et al.*, 2005; George *et al.*, 2009). Positioning rural tourism as a form of sustainable business, Mitchell and Hall (2005), in the introductory chapter of the book they co-edited (Hall *et al.*, 2005), identified the following key themes and issues among the contributions to the edited book: competition; marketing; cooperation and networking; and globalisation.

In many countries, the rural tourism industry is constituted with a great number of small- and medium-sized enterprises (SMEs). There are many practical problems facing these rural tourism business providers. It is important that research in this field should address these problems. Such problems, according to Mitchell and Hall (2005), include:

- lack of concern with and knowledge of demand factors;
- lack of skills with regard to product presentation;
- limited knowledge of the markets; and
- limited development of cooperation and marketing networks.

Research Themes and Issues in Rural Tourism: Chinese Perspectives

Compared to other topics included in this book, the topic of rural tourism is an area that attracted a lot more publications in our review. This may be partly due to the broad nature of rural tourism as a research topic, and partly because of government direction and emphasis on the development of rural tourism. As mentioned by some Chinese scholars, tourism researchers in China tend to follow the government agenda in their research topics selection (Xie, 2003). China has been following a government-led tourism development strategy and the government plays a significant role in China's tourism development (Kuang, 2001). Since the 1990s, the Chinese government has implemented a series of policies and government actions in strategically developing tourism in rural areas and using rural tourism as a lever to relieve poverty in rural areas and achieve rural development goals. After the turn of the century, with the further development of rural tourism industries, the China National Tourism Administration (CNTA), as the central government agency in charge of tourism, set up work guidelines to promote the development of rural tourism. Accordingly, 'China Rural Tourism' and 'China Harmonious City and Countryside Tours' were adopted as the tourism development and promotion themes for 2006 and 2007 (Gao *et al.*, 2009; Yang, 2011). CNTA's emphasis on vigorously developing rural tourism was seen as being in accord with China's national strategy to establish new socialist rural communities in its social and economic transition (Gao *et al.*, 2009).

Government emphasis on rural tourism and its functionality in rural development has possibly guided Chinese researchers' attention towards rural tourism. In 2006, the leading Chinese tourism journal, *Tourism Tribune*, organised written discussions on rural tourism in three consecutive issues (Issues 3–5). Li (2008) indicated that from 2004 to 2007, there were nearly 300 articles on rural tourism published in core Chinese academic journals. In this chapter, our review focuses on the scholarship as demonstrated in relevant publications in the four leading Chinese tourism journals (*Tourism Tribune, Tourism Science, Human Geography* and *Economic Geography*) since 2006.

As rural tourism is a very broad research field, a wide range of topics was found in the published articles. To present a structured and comprehensive review in the following sections, we apply a system typology to classify the issues into supply, demand, and socio-economic issues in relation to rural residents and communities. As noted by Huang and Hsu (2008), tourism researchers in China tended to study supply-side tourism issues more than demand-side tourism issues. This still seems applicable to the research 'landscape' in rural tourism. Generally, we found research issues are around supply-side and macro-management issues rather than demand-side micro-management issues.

Industry Supply-side Research Issues

There are a variety of research topics relevant to industry supply-side issues. These include tourism resources evaluation and planning, rural tourism development models and approaches, industry reintegration, industry systems and stakeholders evaluation.

Resources evaluation and planning

As rural tourism still seems to be a new development option to many underdeveloped regions in China, researchers tend to study the rural tourism resources in specific regions. Understandably, the evaluation of rural tourism resources could be associated with practical tourism planning, in which university-based tourism researchers are often actively involved. For instance, Yin *et al.* (2007) developed a highly quantifiable indicators system in evaluating rural tourism resources in the suburban areas of Shanghai. This system includes resource conditions, development conditions and tourism conditions, each in themselves including detailed sub-criteria with different weightings for assessment. Similarly, Wang and Zhang (2009) used the analytic hierarchy process (AHP) to develop a rural tourism development decision-making model. Factor level indicators in the model are: (1) peripheral attractions; (2) rural characteristics; (3) source market; (4) accessibility; (5) development basis; (6) spatial competitiveness; and (7) sustainable development. A probabilistic model was established based on Delphi inputs and the weightings of the above factors were calculated as 0.035, 0.128, 0.307, 0.236, 0.086, 0.095 and 0.112, respectively. Li (2006) examined the tourism resources and development potentials of the Funiu Mountain region in the southwest of Henan Province and noted different characteristics of the different areas of the mountainous region for its tourism development. Zhu *et al.* (2007) compared the ancient town tourism resources in Anhui and Jiangsu Province. More often, researchers also tend to identify general development problems in rural tourism development (e.g. Long & Zhang, 2006), while taking a macro perspective in examining rural tourism development and its relationship with different types of rural resources such as rural culture (Zhang & Zhang, 2007). In terms of the problems facing rural tourism in China, Long and Zhang (2006) studied the relevant literature and concluded that the problems can be summarised as follows:

- lack of knowledge and understanding of rural tourism among local community, government and rural tourism operators;
- lack of planning;
- insufficient infrastructure for rural tourism development;
- lack of development funds and investment;
- human capacity and management problems; and
- duplicating rural tourism product provisions and unsatisfactory revenue return.

Rural land is an indispensable resource in developing rural tourism. According to Chinese law, rural lands are mostly owned by village collectives but the user rights of lands can be transferred under specific regulations. In the current legislative arrangements on rural lands, there seem to be a lot of practical problems around land use in rural tourism development. Wu *et al.* (2013) developed a risk evaluation framework for rural land utilisation in tourism and the research appears to be practically useful.

As most rural tourism regions cover relatively large rural areas, spatial planning seems important in developing rural tourism. A number of articles attend to spatial planning issues. For instance, applying the 'pole-axis' theory in tourism spatial planning, Xu (2009, 2013) studied the rural tourism spatial structure and agglomeration for Ningbo and Jiangshan in Zhejiang Province. From the landscape ecology perspective, Fan and Li (2009) proposed the 'patch-corridor-matrix-border' pattern in rural tourism planning. While the 'patch' will mostly satisfy the psychological needs for tourist experience, which is the essence of tourism, the 'corridor' will provide the pathway for tourists to reach the core attraction patches, and at the same time function as part of the attraction. Other tourism facilities, infrastructure, and the social and cultural environment will form the major contents of the matrix; at the same time, regional tourism cooperation requires an open-ended rural tourism system in which borders also play important roles in connecting different rural tourism regions. Applying multi-criteria decision analysis (MCDA) and geographic information system (GIS), Zhang and Yang (2009) developed a spatial distribution model for rural tourism development which includes four major evaluation criteria: (1) resources; (2) transportation; (3) economy; and (4) already-developed tourism attractions in the region. The model was applied in the planning of rural tourism development in Ningbo, Zhejiang Province.

Development models and approaches

Different rural development models can be witnessed and identified in China's rural tourism development. In their paper which provides an overview of China's rural tourism, Gao et al. (2009) identified six operational models of rural tourism in China. Table 3.1 summarises these models.

In the Chinese literature, there exist two types of research on the operational models: one evaluating and criticising the current operational models (e.g. Hu et al., 2006) and the other intending to seek more appropriate and ideal development models (e.g. Huang et al., 2006; Zhang et al., 2008; Zhou et al., 2009). The former type seems to attract more research than the latter. As a typical example of the former type, Hu et al.'s (2006) study analysed the Happy Farmers' Home (HFH; Nongjiale in Chinese) operations on the Chongming island of Shanghai and identified the following operational problems:

• The HFH operations are not businesses registered with the relevant industrial and commercial authorities, whereas they should be; this makes the status of these operations illegitimate.

Table 3.1 Operational models of rural tourism in China

Operational model	Description
(1) Corporation plus farmer	Investors set up tourism development corporations and lease land and other resources from farmers to develop tourism attractions and facilities; farmers are involved in the development process by leasing out their land and house buildings, etc.
(2) Corporation plus community plus farmer	Local community as a nexus and base between corporations and farmers.
(3) Government plus corporation plus farmer	Government agencies take the lead to form tourism development corporations or to invite outside investors to develop rural tourism; local farmers join the rural tourism system either by providing tourism-related services or by operating hospitality businesses.
(4) Individual grange	Normally large-scale farmland and associated attractions receiving tourists.
(5) Farmers' cooperatives	Farmers from different service sectors (e.g. dining, accommodation) are engaged and incorporated in cooperative organisations.
(6) Household small business	Small and individual family businesses serving tourists' different needs (e.g. dining, accommodation).

Source: Gao *et al.* (2009: 445).

- Without effective administrative supervision and monitoring, the service and safety standards provided by HFH operations cannot be guaranteed.
- With the rising number of tourist arrivals, the role of village-level organisations becomes increasingly marginalised and cannot effectively resolve administration and industry management problems.
- Due to the unclear prescription of rights and responsibilities of different stakeholders, civil disputes and conflicts are increasing and the general brand image of the island's rural tourism has been damaged.

Ma and colleagues (2007) studied the development practices of Chengdu's (capital city of Sichuan Province in Southwest China) rural tourism development and identified four types of successful development model in rural tourism: (1) village-based rural tourism clustering development; (2) garden-style rural tourism development based on special agricultural industries such as horticulture and gardening; (3) courtyard-style rural tourism development based on leisure and holiday attractions nearby; and (4) development based on ancient towns and folklore and sightseeing resources.

In reality, no development models may be free from problems. However, a small number of scholars would like to explore better development models in China's rural tourism development. For example, Zhou *et al.* (2009), through a comparative analysis of different models of rural tourism development in China (i.e. village led, shareholder company led and cooperative organisation led), argued that exogenous development models relying on external factors would not lead to sustainable tourism development in China; instead, an endogenous development model which situates the local community as the leading and driving force of rural tourism development should be proposed. In another paper, Zhang *et al.* (2008) used actor-network theory (ANT) to deconstruct the actor relations and actions involved in rural tourism development in the Xianhuashan village of Zhejiang Province. This analysis revealed that along the process of development of village tourism, the strong actor has transitioned from farmers in the early stage to tourism authorities in the late stage; such transition has caused the actor network to be less effective in the development process.

While the above-mentioned two studies intended to apply the 'endogenous development theory' to rural tourism development, the mechanisms and conditions that would realise endogenous rural tourism development in China is less clear. As China has a very different political system and rural society system compared to Western countries, the complexity associated with China's rural tourism development should not be underestimated (Huang *et al.*, 2014). In a similar vein, albeit in the English academic language environment, Zou *et al.* (2014) proposed a community-driven endogenous rural tourism development model which includes three mechanisms or operational principles: localisation of supply chain, community-external investor symbiosis, and democratisation of decision-making. In Zou *et al.*'s (2014) study, each principle was evidenced with one case study in the context of rural tourism development in suburban Beijing. These principles are subject to further empirical verification.

Industry reintegration and systems

Naturally, rural tourism may be regarded as a system that connects both the agricultural industry and the tourism industry in rural regions. But surprisingly, little research by tourism researchers in China seems to be directed towards examining how tourism can be integrated with other rural industry sectors. It is speculated that, as all relevant government policies and actions have strongly supported the assumption that rural industries can be facilitated and revived through tourism, and Chinese academics tend to follow the lead of the government (Xie, 2003), there may be little doubt or question among researchers regarding this issue. Nevertheless, such an issue seems to be an important research problem and should be duly examined. As an exceptional case, Yuan (2013) studied the coupling mechanism between agriculture and tourism in China. Using time-series data from 1993 to 2013, based on theories of industry coupling and integration, Yuan's (2013) model indicated that coupling agriculture with tourism (rural tourism) can help increase the productivity of the primary sector and, at the same time, increase the added value of tertiary service sectors other than tourism.

Applying the system theory, rural tourism can also be regarded to be a system composed of subsystems. Understanding the dynamics and the relations among the subsystems is critical to achieving healthy and sustainable development. Yang (2006) deems China's rural tourism system to be composed of four subsystems, namely urban citizens, peasants, the tourism industry and the government. While the desire for 'rurality' from urban residents constitutes the demand of rural tourism, the supply is mainly driven by rural residents' motivation to pursue modern and quality lives. The marketing driving force of rural tourism comes from industry operators' profitability-driven behaviours; the government, on the other hand, plays a significant role in rural tourism development by providing policy and infrastructure support, guided by the national urbanisation and modernisation discourses. However, as noted by Yang (2006), there are a number of conflicts in the rural tourism system. First, the Chinese government's endeavour of eliminating the difference between urban and rural regions is in conflict with the urban residents' 'reversed' touristic pursuit of rurality, which can only exist by preserving the difference between rural and urban. Secondly, while rurality is the foundation of rural tourism, rural residents' desire and actions for a quality modern life on par with their urban counterpart will in effect gradually diminish rurality in any rural regions. Thirdly, the localised small-scale operations taken by local residents will be in conflict with the large-scale profit-driven external capital investors who would seek economy of scale. Fourthly, market-driven/marketised operations for rural tourism will enlarge the gap between the rich and the poor, thus contradicting the government's goal for a common wealth and prosperous society in which members mostly enjoy wealth and good life on relatively equal basis. To effectively resolve the conflicts, Yang (2006) proposed a series of measures which include separating the 'front stage' and 'back stage' production, respecting local communities' benefit-seeking interest in rural tourism, creating a symbiotic industry environment and localised industry supply chain to benefit both external investors and locals, and seeking better institutions, self-governance and organisation among small rural tourism operators.

Multiple stakeholders are involved in the rural tourism system and, as mentioned above, these stakeholders have different interests and expectations in the development process. Zhu (2006) investigated the stakeholders in the rural tourism system, taking the case of Hongsha village in Chengdu, Sichuan Province as an example. The study identified local peasants, urban residents, local government, tourism enterprises and investors (investors may not directly operate tourism businesses) as the major stakeholders in the village's rural development. Tourism products, environmental protection, tourism planning, land development and utilisation were found to be the main issues that the stakeholders are involved in and concerned with. Similarly, Gu (2012) applied the stakeholder theory in her study of rural tourism development in the northwest suburban region of Beijing. In the development process, there have been gaming relationships among the four types of stakeholders, namely local government, local community, tourism companies and tourists. Gu (2012) intended to propose a mechanism in which all stakeholders can share in the benefits of the development. She took a government perspective in developing the stakeholder benefit sharing mechanism. Suggested administration measures include setting up additional government organs to provide public service to the tourism industry, strengthening government regulations and monitoring tourism enterprises' behaviour, and providing fiscal support and transfer to local communities.

From a macro-economic perspective, Chen (2010) proposed the separation of 'back stage' tourism functions from the 'front stage' functions when developing rural tourist experiences to encourage the participation of large tourism corporations in rural tourism. While the 'front stage' of rural tourism can be small, fragmented and representing numerous rural features, the back stage operation can be centralised to reach economies of scale and management with lower costs. Micro-management issues are not commonly studied except for occasional studies on homestay operational resources analysis (Hu, 2007) and electronic commerce applications in rural tourism (Xiong et al., 2006).

Demand-side and Market Issues

There are relatively fewer studies on the topic of demand and market issues than those on supply-side issues as aforementioned in the Chinese tourism literature. Currently, there still seems to be little in-depth understanding of the mass domestic rural tourism market in China. A few comprehensive survey studies illuminate the rural tourist market on a regional basis, for example, Beijing (Wang et al., 2006), Changsha (Su & Huang, 2009;

Su & Wang, 2007), Xi'an (Yang & Li, 2007), and Kunming (Yang & Luo, 2006); as such, they provide fragmented understanding of the markets in these regions. In the survey study conducted by Wang *et al.* (2006) on rural tourism in suburban Beijing, the authors found that the majority of rural tourists were from the 20–50 age range. Forty-five percent of the respondents chose to stay overnight on their trip; a majority of the respondents chose to travel with family (49.7%) or friends (40.2%); 66.1% of the respondents used self-driving as transportation means. In the case of Changsha's suburban region, Su and Wang (2007) found the following rural tourist market characteristics:

- very broad market range for rural tourists in terms of demographics;
- most rural tourists travelling with family and friends;
- word of mouth from relatives and friends as a significant information source for rural tourism;
- self-drive as the major transportation means;
- two hours driving or 200 km as the optimal travel distance;
- leisure and holiday as the main motivation;
- 'rurality' as a concept to attract people who need to release pressure;
- high frequency of rural tourism travel;
- overall high satisfaction with the tourism experience;
- seasonality and winter as the low season;
- high tourist expenditure and market potential; and
- rural features (e.g. idyllic, green, ecological, scenic) as attractions.

These market studies also explored rural tourists' satisfaction levels with different aspects of the rural tourist experience. Wang *et al.* (2006) found that tourists' overall evaluations of accommodation, transportation, outdoor activities and shopping, tourist information and reception service were not high. In the study, respondents found the reception service delivered by local farmers most satisfactory, followed by outdoor activities and shopping; accommodation and transportation were the areas tourists were least satisfied with. In a similar study in Kunming suburb in Yunnan Province, Yang and Luo (2006) found that respondents were most satisfied with sightseeing, followed by rural environment, accommodation and dining; however, they were not satisfied with recreation and outdoor activities, sanitation or the service level. Public transportation services were listed as the least satisfactory item. In Su and Huang's (2009) study, Changsha city residents were found to be most satisfied with accommodation in the suburban rural tourism facilities, followed by dining; shopping and recreation were found to be most unsatisfactory.

Besides these general tourist market studies, some studies examined rural tourists' perceptions of destination features and services in the rural tourism context (Yang & Li, 2007; Yao et al., 2008). Yang and Li (2007) studied Xi'an city residents' perception of rural tourism provisions in the suburbs and found that: (1) rural tourists' preferences for rural attractions demonstrated a regression to nature; and (2) rural tourists had a low evaluation of rural tourism infrastructure and services. Yao et al.'s (2008) study of tourists' perceptions of rural tourism quality in Xiangjiang showed that these perceptions of the service quality of rural tourism were mainly reflections of the rural destination's external overall image, core attractions and resources, reception service attitude and quality, and tourism infrastructure. Other tourist perception studies examined tourists' safety perceptions, and their perceived life pressure and its relationship with leisure adaptation and health (see Gao et al., 2006; Tan et al., 2010). There are also a very small number of marketing studies in the context of rural tourism examining the relationship between tourist satisfaction and loyalty (Su & Huang, 2011), rural tourist destination brand personality and tourist loyalty (Zhang & Bai, 2011), and rural event branding (Lu et al., 2009).

Socio-economic Issues in Rural Tourism

The foundations of Chinese society can be found in rural communities (Fei, 1992). Even with the rapid social and economic transitions and transformations following the opening up and reform eras, the characteristics of China's rural society may still be seen as deeply rooted. Yan (2006, cited by Liu & Jiang, 2011) summarised the characteristics of China's rural society based on Fei's work in the 1930s and 1940s, in five aspects: (1) importance of kinship; (2) relativity in the relationship between public and private, and between a collective group and oneself; (3) self-centred ethical values; (4) social orders being regulated by interpersonal relations and ethics; and (5) a political system of elderly governance. These characteristics seem to be still valid when examining the socio-economic issues in China's rural tourism settings.

In the past decade, many studies in the context of China's rural tourism have addressed socio-economic issues. Specific issues covered in this area are diverse, including community participation and empowerment (e.g. Guo, 2010; Guo & Huang, 2011), social exclusion and residents' rebellion (Guo & Gan, 2011; Zhou, 2012), investment, entrepreneurship, industry cooperation and organisation (Hu, 2009; Huang et al., 2007; Li, 2008), power relationships (Jing & Tyrrell, 2012), development pathways and rural transition (Zhang &

Bao, 2009), governance (Wang, 2009; Xu *et al.*, 2011; Zhu, 2012), and service relations (Yu & Gao, 2009).

Community participation and empowerment

Chinese tourism researchers, especially those based in universities who tend to have a more independent research agenda, are generally concerned with community participation in tourism development. There is a significant body of Chinese literature on community participation as a general topic and Chapter 4 of this volume provides a detailed review of community participation as a generic research topic. In this session, we briefly review some relevant issues with regard to community participation and empowerment in rural tourism.

Local community is one of the major stakeholders in rural tourism, and the community's active involvement and participation in tourism is key to sustainable tourism development (Murphy, 2013). Different issues have been examined by Chinese researchers regarding community participation in rural tourism development. Wang and Hao (2008) applied the AHP in evaluating community participation in rural tourism. Evaluation criteria include social participation, economic participation, cultural participation and decision-making participation. Cao (2012) introduced cultural mapping as a new approach in managing cultural tourism resources in rural communities and encouraging community participation. Cultural mapping, as a development planning technique, includes cultural resource mapping and cultural identity mapping. It is believed that cultural mapping is a useful approach for community participation in rural tourism destinations with a rich cultural heritage.

A few studies examined the factors that may affect community participation. Du and his colleagues found that a perception of belonging to the community, or a sense of community, is closely related to community participation (Du & Su, 2011, 2013; Du *et al.*, 2013). However, it is not clear whether community participation causes this sense of community or if the sense of community leads to community participation. Long (2012) investigated the motivation of women's involvement in rural tourism employment in the developed economic area (Zhongshan city, Guangdong Province) and found that rural females' motivations for working in the tourism sector varied across different sociodemographic strata. The study found that escaping from more demanding jobs, following one's own interests, raising the family income, and setting a good example for the children by working rather than idling were the main motivations for women taking tourism jobs in the region.

In the social system of China's rural society, community participation can also be determined by power relationships. Even as a major stakeholder, local communities may find themselves in a weak power position in interacting with other more powerful stakeholders such as the government and external investors (Bao & Zuo, 2013). Scheyvens (1999) submits that, from a development perspective, community empowerment should be enabled in multiple domains including the social, economic, psychological and political. In the current political system in China, however, rural communities are mostly weak in the political sense. On this basis, some researchers argue that community empowerment is an equally meaningful concept in association with community participation (Sun, 2008; Zuo & Bao, 2008). Based on the case of Yubeng village, in Yunnan Province (also see Chapter 4), Guo (2010) examined the villagers' perceived levels of empowerment under the 'rotation' system of tourist reception. Using Scheyvens' framework, Guo (2010) argued that the four aspects of empowerment were generally achieved with the Yubeng villagers. However, such a case is exceptional as there is no external company involved in Yubeng's development and the villagers collectively control all the tourism operations. Therefore, the empowerment is actually realised at an individual level; however, if external tourism enterprises intervene in the development, it is likely that the benefit sharing system will be broken and damaged. Guo (2010) argued that another form of empowerment, institutional empowerment, should be considered in China's rural tourism development.

In another study, Guo and Huang (2011) investigated the empowerment perceptions of local residents in the Dai Garden of Xishuangbanna, and Yubeng village, both in Yunnan Province. Based on a resident survey, the authors found that in the two communities, economic empowerment was highly acknowledged; however, psychological empowerment, institutional empowerment and information empowerment were low. Residents in Dai Garden scored high on social empowerment, only second to economic empowerment. But Yubeng villagers perceived social empowerment as the lowest. In terms of political empowerment, Yubeng villagers ranked it higher than the Dai Garden community members.

Power and investment relations, entrepreneurship and industry associations

Different power relationships will influence the scenarios of rural tourism and cause variations in the benefit sharing and allocation of the development process. Generally, in China's rural tourism development, the government appears to be the most powerful key stakeholder. Throughout

the development process, residential building relocation and land confisca-
tion are mostly driven by government agencies and these can cause rural
communities to lose their spatial production control rights (Jing & Tyrrell,
2012). Jing and Tyrrell (2012) investigated the power relations in five rural
villages of Taining county in Fujian Province. They found that both the tourism spatial planning structure and the community power structure can
influence a community's benefit sharing from tourism. However, community power seems more important, as without such power in dealing with
the government, a community may lose the right to control their own community space so as to benefit from tourism production. In a rural community, a small number of social and economic elites can make the community
more powerful in dealing with government interventions. We will further
discuss elite governance in the 'governance' section that follows.

Social conflict is commonly witnessed in China's rural development.
Many case studies, including the cases presented in Chapter 4 of this book,
indicate that social conflicts mainly occur between local residents and tourism companies/local government. Some studies have recorded phenomena in
relation to such conflicts. Zhou (2012) documented the daily resistance of
villagers from an ancient town in Anhui Province. Dissatisfied with the
inequality in tourism benefit sharing, the villagers would demolish their old
houses and build new modern-style homes in order to express their resistance. Guo and Gan (2011) investigated the perceived social exclusion among
local villagers in Wuyuan, Jiangxi Province. It was found that changes
brought about by tourism development created feelings of frustration and
low self-esteem among villagers. Villagers perceived their social exclusion in
terms of economic, political, cultural and relationship exclusion.

Many rural tourism destinations in China face capital constraints in
tourism development. As in any other development context, investment is
important. Many parties could invest in rural tourism, with different scales
and intentions. Rural tourism investment could involve local government,
external investors, village collectives or individual households in the village. Huang et al. (2007) analysed the relationships among all these different types of investor, based on the case of the Songlan Mountain tourism
resort in Zhejiang Province. In the case study, it was found that different
types of investors play different roles in rural tourism. Government investment is mainly in the construction of infrastructural facilities, such as
transportation, telecommunications, sewage disposal, environmental protection, and so on. The scale of government investment is large but has low
efficiency. The local county government takes charge of ticketing for the
Songlan Mountain tourism resort and treats this income as non-tax government revenue. External investors usually place their interest and

investment into large projects like hotels or outdoor sports and hunting facilities, whereas the local community and community members generally invest in small service projects like tourist shops and parking lots. Huang *et al.* (2007) found that the level of marketisation in rural tourism investment in the case study is high. Government, external investors and the local community and its members differentiate their investment focuses in the tourism system and follow the market economy principles in rural tourism development.

While local community-based entrepreneurship is important in rural tourism development, considering that most local rural tourism businesses are small and medium-sized enterprises (SMEs), entrepreneurship is not commonly found in the Chinese rural tourism literature. The exception is Li's (2008) study. Li (2008) studied the factors that influence local rural tourism operators' entrepreneurial behaviour. It was found these factors included: (1) increasing family income; (2) self-actualisation; (3) sustaining household life needs; (4) fulfilling their own personal interests; (5) external support; and (6) investment risk. The study applied Getz and Carlsen's (2000) 12-item family business goals scale in the tourism context and found that monetary incentives and the encouragement of family/friends seemed to be most influential in starting up small rural tourism businesses.

China has a unique government arrangement at its grass-root levels (township and village). There are various ways of organising industry associations made up of rural household-based businesses. Cooperative organisations and associations at village level that bring together individual family businesses demonstrated various forms, patterns and models. Some of these cooperative organisations seemed to have inherited similar rural operative systems from the old days of the socialist planning economy (Zhou & Jiang, 2013). It can be observed that research on industry clustering and networking in China's rural tourism context is very limited. Somehow, industry clustering and networking research may be overshadowed by studies on industry cooperative associations, which appear to have a higher number of publications.

Hu (2009) reviewed the development of rural tourism industry association in China and noted the following four categories of industry cooperative organisations:

- Happy Farmers' Home (HFH) service centres, which are often set up by township governments and take an independent legal-person status in their operation. These service centres also contribute to the standardisation of services and management in the region's rural tourism development.

- Associations of HFH operations; these are self-regulating management organisations among individual HFH businesses and are mostly encouraged and supported by the local government.
- Tourism service companies established by village or township government which cooperate with relevant rural tourism businesses and individual HFH households and share the revenue with them.
- HFH cooperatives, which are legal-person business entities incorporated with five or more individuals under the *Act of Rural Professional Cooperatives* promulgated on 1 July 2007.

Development pathways, governance and service relations

Rural tourism in China is still rapidly developing, and the development paths and patterns in China's grand rural transition are not clear. Applying the path-dependence theory from neo-institutional economics and referring to Butler's tourism area life cycle (TALC) model, Zhang and Bao (2009) presented their 'origin-dynamics' conceptual framework for the development of rural tourism. There are two propositions:

- The pathway of a rural community's tourism development will be determined by its specific 'origin', that is, the initial state of the rural community's development before developing tourism, including historical endowment (e.g. natural resources, cultural heritage, and social and economic development), and those random events facilitating tourism development.
- The pathway of a rural community's tourism development will be determined by the specific dynamics as defined by the complex interactions and mutual influences in factors like the natural environment, social, economic, cultural and political systems.

The origin-dynamics framework provides a useful analytical approach to examining micro rural development cases. Zhang and Bao (2009) applied the framework in analysing Xidi's development path and the application demonstrates that the conceptual framework is a useful supplement to TALC.

Many researchers have noted that in a rural community elite members play an important role in tourism development. Wang (2009) studied community participation in tourism and heritage protection in Pingan village, in Guangxi Province, and argued that elite governance together with government intervention and external investor involvement is the optimal arrangement for heritage-based rural tourism development. In the case of the Tiger Leaping Gorge Hiking Route development in Yunnan Province, Zhu (2012) found that a new type of rural elite was generated during the rural development process. These elites are those who accumulate personal wealth and corresponding social power through entrepreneurial involvement in tourism-related businesses. They are different from the traditional type of rural elites who rely more on political status and personal networks. The new elites had in-depth interaction with foreign backpacker travellers in the region and assimilated sustainable development values and ideologies in their business practices. They in turn become more powerful politically and socially by citizenship behaviours like donating to improve public infrastructure, and working to protect local interests. However, these new elites do not seem to be politically united and their influence within the existing local social structure is therefore limited.

Elite governance models are only mentioned in the literature as one of many existing models in rural tourism development. Many issues around elite governance, such as how the elites can share the power with a strong government, have not yet been clearly answered. In terms of rural tourism governance, researchers also propose that a polycentric governance model may be applied to managing rural tourism resources in order to achieve sustainable development. For instance, Xu *et al.* (2010) argued that, based on the classification of different rural tourism resources (i.e. public, collective, private), a polycentric governance model including government, rural residents, tourism enterprises, media and academics could be applied.

The service relation between host and guests in China's rural tourism context is an interesting social and economic phenomenon. Yu and Gao (2009) noted that – in contrast to the service delivery in other contexts which is characterised by predetermined service components and arrangements – rural tourism services are usually centred around customers' personalised needs and demonstrate a large degree of flexibility towards customers. In such a service delivery process, service providers transfer the service control right to their customers. In essence, such a transfer of service delivery control redefines the service relationship between the service provider and the consumer.

Conclusion

This chapter provides a comprehensive review of the Chinese literature on rural tourism development. There is a significant body of literature in Chinese on this subject. There are many research topics in relation to rural tourism, covering industry supply, demand and complex socio-economic issues. More research attention has been directed towards the supply-side and social issues than the demand-side issues. There are many case studies examining community participation and empowerment. It is believed that these case studies can greatly enrich the literature on community-based tourism (CBT) in the international tourism research community. A comparative meta-analysis on community participation cases in and outside China may be especially useful as a future research endeavour.

While it is not our intention to provide a point-to-point comparison between the English and Chinese rural tourism literature, it is worth noting that while there are a significant number of studies on inter-sector industry clustering, cooperation and networking in the English literature, there are few such studies in the Chinese literature. However, it should be noted that some rural tourism development models seem to have inherited features from China's past socialist rural economy system (e.g. the communal model in Zhou & Jiang, 2013). These socialist institutional arrangements, above all, may provide an alternative approach to guarantee tourism development benefit sharing among the stakeholders. As such, industry practices in China rural tourism may provide cases and empirical evidence to enrich the literature in rural tourism as a whole.

There are still a lot of research issues that seem to be important but have not been covered in any depth in the Chinese literature. These include marketing issues, destination branding, regional marketing cooperation and rural tourist market segmentation. Most of these issues are on the demand side and should be further addressed. Also, maintaining 'authenticity' seems to be critical in the experiences that rural tourists seek and enables sustainable rural tourism development (Xu *et al.* 2011); thus the concepts of authenticity and rurality should be critically re-evaluated in the context of China's urbanisation and modernisation process. Oakes (2013) remarks that, with the influences of urbanisation and globalisation, rurality and rural culture are fast disappearing. In China, rural villages with history and cultural heritage are being museumised one after another. Villages become urbanites' playgrounds. Young people are being forced out of their home villages due to life pressures and their social identity is endangered. More critical studies need to be conducted about social equity, inclusion and rural community well-being issues.

References

Bao, J. and Zuo, B. (2013) Institutional opportunism in tourism investment. In C. Ryan and S. Huang (eds) *Tourism in China: Destinations, Planning and Experiences* (pp. 38–54). Bristol: Channel View Publications.

Bloomberg (2012) China's urban population exceeds countryside for first time. *Bloomberg. com*, 17 January. See http://www.bloomberg.com/news/2012-01-17/china-urban-population-exceeds-rural.html (accessed 12 January 2015).

Cao, X. (2012) Cultural mapping: A new method of community involvement and the practice in cultural rural tourism. *Tourism Tribune* 27 (2), 67–73.

Chen, J. (2010) Research on structure of collectivization operations in country tourism based on front-back stage decoupling. *Economic Geography* 30 (8), 1378–1382.

Du, Z. and Su, Q. (2011) Study on the relationship between the community participation of rural tourism, residents' perceived tourism impact and sense of community involvement – a case study of Anji rural tourism destination, Zhejiang Province. *Tourism Tribune* 26 (11), 65–70.

Du, Z. and Su, Q. (2013) Influence of sense of community on community involvement in rural tourism destination: A case study of Anji County in Zhejiang Province. *Tourism Science* 27 (3), 61–71.

Du, Z., Su, Q. and Jiang, L. (2013) A structural model of residents' sense of community in rural tourism destinations and its application: A case study of Anji County in Zhejiang Province. *Tourism Tribune* 28 (6), 65–74.

Fan, C. and Li, B. (2009) Spatial pattern of countryside tourism based on the theory of landscape ecology. *Economic Geography* 29 (4), 683–687.

Fei, X. (1992) *From the Soil: The Foundations of Chinese Society*. Los Angeles, CA: University of Chicago Press.

Gannon, A. (1994) Rural tourism as a factor in rural community economic development for economies in transition. *Journal of Sustainable Tourism* 2 (1–2), 51–60.

Gao, P., Yao, H. and Zhou, L. (2006) Empirical research on the rural tourists' safety cognition. *Economic Geography* 26 (12), 35–37.

Gao, S., Huang, S. and Huang, Y. (2009) Rural tourism development in China. *International Journal of Tourism Research* 11 (5), 439–450.

Gartner, W.C. (2004) Rural tourism development in the USA. *International Journal of Tourism Research* 6, 151–164.

George, E.W., Mair, H. and Reid, D.G. (2009) *Rural Tourism Development: Localism and Cultural Change*. Bristol: Channel View Publications.

Getz, D. and Carlsen, J. (2000) Characteristics and goals of family and owner-operated businesses in the rural tourism and hospitality sectors. *Tourism Management* 21, 547–560.

Greffe, X. (1994) Is rural tourism a lever for economic and social development? *Journal of Sustainable Tourism* 2 (1–2), 22–40.

Gu, H. (2012) Study on the development of rural tourism and construction of rural residents' interest-sharing mechanism – a case of the development of tourism industry in the Northwest area of Haidian District, Beijing. *Tourism Tribune* 27 (1), 26–30.

Guo, H. and Gan, Q. (2011) Rural tourism community residents' multi-dimensional perception of social exclusion – a qualitative research on the case of Likeng village in Wuyuan, Jiangxi Province. *Tourism Tribune* 26 (8), 87–94.

Guo, W. (2010) Study on the 'Alternative system mode' regarding rural residents' participation in tourism development and community empowerment effectiveness. *Tourism Tribune* 25 (3), 76–83.

Guo, W. and Huang, Z. (2011) Study on the development of community power and functions under the background of the development of rural tourism – based on the investigation of two typical cases in Daizu Garden and Yubeng Community. *Tourism Tribune* 26 (12), 83–92.

Hall, D.R., Kirkpatrick, I. and Mitchell, M. (2005) *Rural Tourism and Sustainable Business*. Clevedon: Channel View Publications.

Hu, M. (2007) An analysis of the core resources in the management of rural lodgings. *Tourism Tribune* 22 (9), 64–69.

Hu, M. (2009) On the development and transition of China's rural tourism specialised cooperative organisations – the upgrade of rural tourism development mode. *Tourism Tribune* 24 (2), 70–74.

Hu, X., Li, B. and Niu, J. (2006) On the drawbacks of the existing tourist operation mode of 'Happy Farm Households Tour' in Chongming Island and study of innovation. *Tourism Tribune* 21 (5), 28–32.

Huang, L., Lu, L. and Ding, Y. (2006) A research on the tourism development model in ethnic minority village – taking Xishuangbanna Dai Park as an example. *Tourism Tribune* 21 (5), 53–56.

Huang, S. and Hsu, C.H.C. (2008) Recent tourism and hospitality research in China. *International Journal of Hospitality & Tourism Administration* 9 (3), 267–287.

Huang, S., van der Veen, R. and Zhang, G. (2014) Editorial essay: new era of China tourism research. *Journal of China Tourism Research* 10 (4), 379–387.

Huang, Y., Zhang, G. and Li, J. (2007) A study of the relationship between investors in rural tourism. *Tourism Tribune* 22 (6), 75–79.

Jing, X. and Tyrrell, T.J. (2012) Power relationship, community space and benefit gaining from rural tours: an empirical study based on five tourist rural communities of Taining County in Fujian Province. *Tourism Science* 26 (5), 20–29.

Kuang, L. (2001) *Study on the Tourism Industry Government Led Development Strategy.* Beijing: China Tourism Press.

Lane, B. (1994) What is rural tourism? *Journal of Sustainable Tourism* 2 (1–2), 7–21.

Li, R. (2006) Analysis on spatial difference of tourism development in Funiu Mountain. *Economic Geography* 26 (3), 538–540.

Li, X. (2008) A study on the influencing factors of starting rural tourism businesses. *Tourism Tribune* 23 (1), 19–25.

Lin, Q. and Dai, W. (2006) The interaction between rural tourism and rural area development. *Economic Geography* 26 (12), 31–34.

Liu, W. and Jiang, J. (2011) The research framework for the impact of tourism development on the society and culture of rural ethnic communities. *Economic Geography* 31 (6), 1025–1030.

Long, L. (2012) Study on the motivations of rural women's participation in rural tourism in economy developed areas – a case study of Xinlun village, Zhongshan City. *Tourism Tribune* 27 (2), 37–42.

Long, M. and Zhang, H. (2006) An analysis and resolution of the problems existing in rural tourism. *Tourism Tribune* 21 (9), 75–79.

Lu, Z., Zhang, W. and Tang, J. (2009) An empirical study on brand image of rural festival tourist activities – a case of Luoping Rape Bloom Festival. *Tourism Tribune* 24 (5), 61–66.

Ma, Y., Zhao, L., Song, H., Guo, Q. and Liu, M. (2007) Study on the Chinese rural tourism development pattern – a case of Chengdu. *Economic Geography* 27 (2), 336–339.

Mitchell, M. and Hall, D. (2005) Rural tourism as sustainable business: Key themes and issues. In D.R. Hall, I. Kirkpatrick and M. Mitchell (eds) *Rural Tourism and Sustainable Business* (pp. 3–14). Clevedon: Channel View Publications.

Murphy, P.E. (2013) *Tourism: A Community Approach* (4th edn). New York: Routledge.

Oakes, T. (2013) Written discussion – villages: The amusement part of Chinese cities. *Tourism Tribune* 28 (4), 3–6.

Roberts, L. and Hall, D. (2001) *Rural Tourism and Recreation: Principles to Practice.* Wallingford: CABI.

Scheyvens, R. (1999) Ecotourism and the empowerment of local communities. *Tourism Management* 20, 245–249.

Sharpley, R. and Roberts, L. (2004) Rural tourism – 10 years on. *International Journal of Tourism Research* 6, 119–124.

Su, L. and Huang, F. (2009) An empirical study on rural tour satisfaction of urban residents: A case study of Changsha. *Tourism Science* 23 (4), 42–49.

Su, L. and Huang, F. (2011) Study on the relationship between tourists' satisfaction and loyalty – a comparative analysis of sightseeing tourists and rural tourists. *Tourism Tribune* 26 (11), 39–45.

Su, L. and Wang, L. (2007) On the characteristics of rural tourism market in the periphery of cities – a case study of Changsha. *Tourism Tribune* 22 (2), 67–71.

Sun, J. (2008) Empowerment theory and the construction of community capability in the development of tourism. *Tourism Tribune* 23 (9), 22–27.

Tan, J., Tang, J. and Song, J. (2010) On the relationships between rural tourists' life stress, leisure coping strategies and health. *Tourism Tribune* 25 (2), 66–71.

Wang, B., Luo, Z. and Hao, S. (2006) A study on the current situation of the development of rural tourism in Beijing. *Tourism Tribune* 21 (10), 63–69.

Wang, F. and Hao, X. (2008) Evaluation of community participation in rural tourism areas based on analytic Hierarchy process – taking Diaowo village, Pinggu District, Beijing as an example. *Tourism Tribune* 23 (8), 52–57.

Wang, L. (2009) On the elite governance of cultural heritage in rural tourism communities – discussion about the election in Pingan Stockaded Village, Guangxi Province. *Tourism Tribune* 24 (5), 67–71.

Wang, T. and Zhang, X. (2009) Study on development decision-making path of recreational belt around metropolis (ReBAM) rural tourism based on probability model. *Tourism Tribune* 24 (11), 30–35.

Wu, G., Niu, X. and Xu, H. (2013) Study on land transfer risk evaluation during the development of rural tourism. *Economic Geography* 33 (3), 187–191.

Xie, Y. (2003) Tourism and hospitality industry studies: A comparative research between China and the overseas countries. *Tourism Tribune* 18 (5), 20–25.

Xiong, J., Liu, C. and Yuan, J. (2006) On e-commerce development and its network system construction of rural tourism. *Economic Geography* 26 (2), 340–345.

Xu, F., Qin, X. and Li, Q. (2010) Research on polycentric governance of rural tourism destination supported by resources system. *Tourism Science* 24 (2), 18–25.

Xu, F., Lu, Q., Qin, X. and Yang, X. (2011) Research on sustainable development of rural tourist economy: An authenticity perspective. *Tourism Science* 25 (1), 26–34.

Xu, Q. (2009) The spatial construction optimization of Ningbo's rural tourism based on the pole-axis system theory. *Economic Geography* 29 (6), 1042–1046.

Xu, Q. (2013) Research on spatial agglomeration of rural tourism based on the 'pole-axis system' theory – a case study of Jiangshan in Zhejiang Province. *Economic Geography* 33 (4), 174–178.

Yang, A. (2011) Written discussion: Improving and updating rural tourism from an industry integration perspective. *Tourism Tribune* 26 (4), 9–11.

Yang, J. (2006) A study of the driving factors of rural tourism in China and the systematic optimization. *Tourism Science* 20 (4), 7–11.

Yang, M. and Luo, J. (2006) Survey and research on the rural ecotourism and Tuanjie village in Kunming City. *Tourism Tribune* 21 (2), 51–55.

Yang, Y. and Li, T. (2007) A study on the development of rural tourist destination in Xi'an based on the evaluation of tourists' psychological perception. *Tourism Tribune* 22 (11), 32–37.

Yao, J., Chen, B. and Tian, S. (2008) Study on tourists' perception of rural travel quality in ethnic region – a case study of Dushi Farm, Changji Prefecture, Xinjiang. *Tourism Tribune* 23 (11), 75–81.

Yin, Z., Yin, J. and Xu, S. (2007) A study on the quantitative evaluation of rural tourism resources in Shanghai. *Tourism Tribune* 22 (8), 59–63.

Yu, K. and Gao, Y. (2009) The discussion on service control transfer phenomenon in rural tourism. *Economic Geography* 29 (12), 2085–2089.

Yuan, Z. (2013) Dynamic effects and development tendency of coupling between rural tourism industry and big agriculture. *Tourism Tribune* 28 (5), 80–88.

Zhang, C. and Bai, K. (2011) Brand personality of rural tourism destinations and tourists' loyalty: Mediating effect of place attachment. *Tourism Tribune* 26 (2), 49–57.

Zhang, H. and Yang, Q. (2009) Spatial distribution of rural tourism for construction of new country based on MCDA. *Human Geography* 3, 75–79.

Zhang, H., Zhou, Y., Wei, H. and Huang, C. (2008) An empirical study of rural tourism endogenous development based on actor-network theory – a case of Xianhuashan village. *Tourism Tribune* 23 (2), 65–71.

Zhang, X. and Bao, J. (2009) Tourism development and rural vicissitudes: The hypothesis of 'origin-dynamics'. *Tourism Tribune* 24 (6), 19–24.

Zhang, Y. and Zhang, Y. (2007) Rural culture and development of rural tourism. *Economic Geography* 27 (3), 509–512.

Zhou, C. (2012) Residents' daily resistance in rural tourism destinations – a case study of disturbances concerning tearing down and building houses in Hui village. *Tourism Tribune* 27 (2), 32–36.

Zhou, Y. and Jiang, Y. (2013) A model of mountain region rural tourism development: The case of Suichang. In C. Ryan and S. Huang (eds) *Tourism in China: Destinations, Planning and Experiences* (pp. 22–37). Bristol: Channel View Publications.

Zhou, Y., Jiang, J. and Wang, X. (2009) A study of community-driven endogenous rural tourism development model. *Tourism Science* 23 (4), 36–41.

Zhu, H. (2006) On the theory of rural tourism stakeholders in China – a case study on the Hongsha Village in Chengdu. *Tourism Tribune* 21 (5), 23–27.

Zhu, X. (2012) A research on the forming and acting mechanism of new rural economic elites in rural tourism: Based on a case study of Tiger Leaping George Hiking Route in Yunnan, China. *Tourism Tribune* 27 (6), 73–78.

Zhu, X., Lu, L. and Li, Z. (2007) Comparative study on tourism development of traditional village and town resorts – a comparative analysis of Huizhou ancient village buildings and six old towns in southern area of Yantze River tourism development. *Economic Geography* 27 (5), 842–846.

Zou, T., Huang, S. and Ding, P. (2014) Towards a community-driven development model of rural tourism: The Chinese experience. *International Journal of Tourism Research* 16 (3), 261–271.

Zuo, B. and Bao, J. (2008) From community participation to community empowerment – review on theoretical study of 'Tourism Empowerment' in Western countries. *Tourism Tribune* 23 (4), 58–63.

4 Community Participation and Involvement in Tourism: Cases and Models in China

Introduction

Over the past 30 years since the reform and opening up eras, China has undergone tremendous transformation in various aspects, most prominently in political decentralisation (Cao, 2011; Walder, 1995; Zhou, 2006), marketisation of the economy (Zhang, 2008, 2010) and civil society development (O'Brien & Li, 2006; Sofield & Li, 1998, 2011). These form the national background for community participation and involvement in tourism in China. Community participation in the tourism development process (TDP) in China is significantly different from that in Western countries. The differences are reflected in many respects, including the social meaning of community participation, the benefit for the community members, and power relations among the stakeholders (e.g. Bao & Sun, 2006; Bao & Zuo, 2012; Li, 2004, 2006; Sofield & Li, 1998, 2011; Ying & Zhou, 2007). In recent years, tourism researchers in China have examined and summarised different models of community participation and involvement in the TDP, mostly within ethnic and rural tourism contexts. A good number of cases have been presented in published articles. These studies are reviewed and presented in this chapter to provide a knowledge base to understand tourism development in China.

Models and Cases of Community Participation in the Tourism Development Process in China

Many past studies have provided useful clues and indicators in developing a typology of community participation in the TDP. Scheyvens' (1999) framework for analysing the empowerment of local communities (economic, psychological, social and political empowerment), although not a specialised typology of community participation, provides good guidance in classifying studies in the area of community participation in the TDP. Timothy (1999: 372) views benefit sharing and decision-making as two essential standards by which local community's participation in the TDP should be examined. Based on the differences of local communities' participation levels in the TDP, Tosun (1999) identified three types of community participation in the context of tourism development: (1) *spontaneous participation,* which is at the high end of the participation continuum; in such a process, participants are self-motivated and are actively involved in benefit sharing and decision-making; (2) *passive participation,* in which local communities' roles in tourism development are limited to their performing assigned tasks as decision-takers, not decision-makers; and (3) *pseudo participation,* which is a top-down and mostly indirect form and could be seen as going towards non-participation. In pseudo participation, no opportunity is given to host communities to have a voice in the decision-making process of tourism development. Adopting two dimensions from Bramwell and Sharman's (2000) framework, *scope of community participation* and *intensity of community participation,* Li et al. (2007) established a 'scope-intensity matrix' which identified five community participation scenarios. In this matrix, scope of participation varies from exclusion to partial participation to full participation, while intensity of participation differs at levels of exclusion, passive participation or active participation.

Although the extent (e.g. scope, level, depth and intensity, among other terms used) to which local community members participate in the TDP has been extensively studied, the issue of power relationships (the degree of power distribution) among the stakeholders in tourism development in China remains not well addressed. As a matter of fact, power relationships have been commonly used as a criterion in distinguishing different scenarios (scopes, levels, depth and intensity) of community participation in the TDP in the literature (e.g. Bahaire & Elliott-White, 1999; Hung *et al.,* 2011; Tosun, 1999, 2000, 2006). Therefore, it is necessary to consider the concept of power relationships among stakeholders in developing a typology of community participation in the TDP in China. In China, governments, enterprises and

		Dominating stakeholder		
		Local government	*Tourism enterprise*	*Local community*
Participation extent	*High full*	Full participation in government-dominated development	Full participation in enterprise-dominated development	Full participation in community-dominated development
	Low limited	Limited participation in government-dominated tourism development	Limited participation in enterprise-dominated development	Limited participation in community-dominated development

Figure 4.1 A typology of community participation in tourism development in China

local communities are involved in the TDP as major stakeholders (e.g. Bao & Sun, 2006; Bao & Zuo, 2012; Sofield & Li, 1998, 2011). Tourism developments in different regions could be characterised by a particular stakeholder dominating the TDP; this has been noted by some scholars either as the community-dominated model (e.g. Yu, 2008; Zhou *et al.*, 2009), or the enterprise-dominated model (e.g. Liu *et al.*, 2008), respectively. In this chapter, we intend to develop a typology of community participation models in tourism by adopting power relationships among stakeholders and the extent (e.g. scope, level, depth, intensity) to which community members participate in the TDP as two basic criteria (see Figure 4.1). In this typology, four models of community participation in the TDP are identified in the tourism literature in Chinese. They are: (1) limited participation in government-dominated development; (2) limited participation in enterprise-dominated development; (3) limited participation in community-dominated development; and (4) full participation in community-dominated development, respectively. In this typology, 'limited participation' generally refers to inadequate participation in terms of scope (e.g. the number of community members), intensity (the level/depth of participation), or both. The characteristics and representative cases of each of the identified models are elaborated below.

Limited Participation in Government-dominated Tourism Development

Under such a model, local government or the administrative authority of a tourism area plays a dominating role in the TDP, controlling its decision-making process, while the local community can only participate in and benefit from tourism development in a very limited way. Usually, the local government sets up companies that they fully own and/or control to deal with business-related issues; tourism development under such circumstances is therefore still government dominated. The Hongkeng village in Yongding County, Fujian Province (Yan & Zhang, 2008) and the Diaolou (fortified tower houses) villages in Kaiping City, Guangdong Province (Wang & Huang, 2013) are two representative cases that illustrate this community participation model.

The Hongkeng village case

The Yongding Tulou (Hakka Earth Building) Folk and Cultural Village (the YTFCV) is located in Hongkeng village. A *tulou* is usually a large, enclosed and fortified rectangular or circular earth building with very thick load-bearing rammed earth walls. A typical *tulou* has three to five storeys and can house up to 80 families. Hongkeng village occupies an area of about 2.5 km^2, with a registered population of about 2300 (more than 500 households). However, about half of the registered residents, mainly males and young villagers, earn a living and support their families as peasant workers away from the village. Early in 1993, the government of Yongding County began tourism development in the village, and established the YTFCV, charging admission fees at the entrance of the village. In 2001 the government of Yongding County set up the Yongding Tulou Tourism Development Company and authorised it to take full charge of development and management issues in the YTFCV. Meanwhile, the Yongding County Tourism Bureau, the township government of Hukeng under which Hongkeng village is administered, and the Hongkeng Villagers' Committee[1] have supporting roles. For instance, the Hongkeng Villagers' Committee is intended to support the Yongding County Land Bureau in requisitioning local villagers' lands and houses for use in tourism development.

In this case, all the income from admission fees becomes the county government's fiscal revenue; the county government, however, reallocates some revenue back to the Yongding Tulou Tourism Development Company as funds designated for the promotion, management and maintenance of the *tulou* buildings (Yan & Zhang, 2008). Among the more than 20 *tulou* buildings in the village, five are rented and included as major attractions of the YTFCV. So the villagers who live in these five buildings can get rentals from the company and sell local crafts to visitors or run catering businesses. According to a survey (cited in Yan & Zhang, 2008), villagers living in these five buildings are more involved in tourism development than other villagers; about three-quarters of these villagers participated in tourism development. During the development process, some villagers were reallocated outside the village; although they were compensated by the county government, they lost out on the opportunity to participate in tourism development. It is common to see villagers who did not rent out their *tulou* buildings operating tourism-related small businesses like selling crafts or running homestays and restaurants.

Although the villagers can participate in and benefit from tourism development through the above-mentioned approaches, they are mostly excluded from the decision-making (e.g. tourism planning and daily management) (Yan & Zhang, 2008). Since the company is fully owned and controlled by the county government, all the management employees are appointed by the government. Positions with higher salaries, such as security guards and tour guides, are staffed by people from outside the village. Local villagers are mostly employed as cleaners (Yan & Zhang, 2008).

The Kaiping Diaolou villages case

Four villages in Kaiping (Guangdong Province, Southern China) can also be taken as a case study to showcase the characteristics of community participation in government-dominated tourism development. These villages have been designated as a UN Educational, Scientific and Cultural Organization (UNESCO) World Heritage site, because of their *diaolou* buildings (late 19th-century defensive towers). Similar to the above-discussed Hongkeng village case, the municipal government in Kaiping established a fully owned and controlled company in 2010, the Guangdong Kaiping Diaolou Tourism Development Company (the GKDTDC), and authorised it to take full responsibility for the tourism development and management issues at the World Heritage site. According to Wang and Huang (2013), local villagers participate in tourism development and gain benefit in the following ways. First, about 30 villagers from three of the four villages are employed by the GKDTDC as security guards, cleaners and maintenance staff. Secondly, some villagers operate stalls selling souvenirs, crafts and local agricultural products, while others choose to run home-based restaurants. Thirdly, residents in two villages receive shares from the GKDTDC's tourism revenues. In the Majianglong Administrative Village, when an admission ticket of 50 RMB is sold by the GKDTDC, 0.5 RMB and 4.5 RMB will be given to the local township government and the village, respectively. Subsequently, in the village share, 4 RMB will be allocated to villagers and 0.5 RMB to the Villagers' Committee; of this 4 RMB, 3.5 RMB goes to the five natural villages that are included in the UNESCO World Heritage site and 0.5 RMB to the two natural villages that are not included. In 2009, each Majianglong villager received 400 RMB from admission ticket revenues.

However, in the development process, villagers have rarely been involved in decision-making. According to a survey conducted by Wang and Huang (2013), only 11% of the interviewed villagers reported that they had been involved in decision-making and planning issues relating to tourism development; more than 70% of them had not received any tourism-related training; nearly 65% did not know how to report to governmental agencies about tourism development issues; and nearly 90% did not think that the local government could resolve the problems they reported. Therefore, similar to the case of Hongkeng village, although local villagers can participate in tourism development and gain benefit from it in limited ways, they are excluded from the decision-making process.

To sum up, the above two cases highlight a scenario as illustrated by Li *et al.* (2007: 123). In such a scenario, some community members can share economic benefits through renting out houses or taking low-paid and unstable menial jobs related to the TDP, but they are mostly kept away from decision-making in the TDP.

Limited Participation in Enterprise-dominated Development

Under enterprise-dominated tourism development, an external company usually plays a dominating role and controls the decision-making process in tourism development, while the local community can only participate in tourism and benefit from it in very limited ways. This situation is very similar to the above-mentioned two cases in the government-dominated tourism developments. The Daizu Garden in Xishuangbanna, Yunnan Province (e.g. Guo & Huang, 2011; Zuo & Bao, 2012) and Hongcun village in Yixian County, Anhui Province (e.g. Jiang *et al.*, 2009; Lu *et al.*, 2010; Yu *et al.*, 2013) are representative cases.

The Daizu Garden case

The Daizu Garden consists of five adjacent Dai villages (natural villages) with a total population of 1617 (339 households). It is located in Jinghong, the capital city of Xishuangbanna Prefecture, Yunnan Province. Tourism development in the five villages, now combined into an integral tourism area, dates back to 1988. In 1998, a Guangdong-based company signed a cooperation contract with the local government of Jinghong. With this contract, the company established the Xishuangbanna Daizu Garden Company (the XDGC), and encircled the five villages to form the Daizu Garden (Zuo &

Bao, 2012). The five villages then became the tourist attractions featuring the Dai culture (e.g. Dai folk customs, architecture and cuisine) and Buddhist culture in the Daizu Garden. The company sells admission tickets to tourists (Guo & Huang, 2011). In the Daizu Garden, community participation follows the so-called 'company + community' model (Zuo & Bao, 2012). In such a model, the villagers provide and produce the attractions (e.g. cultural performance, dance) to tourists, while the company builds and maintains the infrastructure and tourism facilities, and organises cultural performances (Guo & Huang, 2011; Zuo & Bao, 2012). In 2009, more than 5 million tourists visited the Daizu Garden, making it the second largest tourist area in terms of tourist arrivals in the Xishuangbanna Prefecture (Zuo & Bao, 2012).

In the 'company + community' model, admission fees and income from other related businesses belong to the XDGC. The lands used for tourism development by the company are rented from the Villagers' Committee (for collectively owned lands) and individual villagers (for household-contracted lands). By the end of 2009, about 930 acres of land were rented, representing 5.5% of the total area of the Daizu Garden (Zuo & Bao, 2012). The five village communities participate in tourism development and gain benefits in the following ways (Guo & Huang, 2011; Zuo & Bao, 2012). First, households whose lands are rented can obtain land rents and related compensation. The initial land rents, starting in 1999, were 300 RMB per mu per year. Secondly, the five villages together are paid 95,000 RBM per year to preserve the traditional wooden dry-column buildings and Buddhist temples, which form the core attractions for tourists. In addition, the company also subsidises 4000 RMB to each household that has built and/or repaired their traditional Dai buildings. By the end of 2009, the company had spent 600,000 RMB on such a programme. Thirdly, more than 600 local villagers, or 37% of the total villagers, are employed in the tourism sector, either working as tour guides and dance performers, or running *Daijiale* (Dai farm stays) and souvenir shops (Zuo & Bao, 2012). Fourthly, seniors and low-income families can receive a living allowance, and college students from low-income families can obtain stipends from the company on a regular basis.

In spite of the above-mentioned participation and benefits, increasing tensions and conflicts between local villagers and the company have been recorded in recent years. For instance, in the Dai New Year of 2007, all the villagers declined the beef that the company allocated to each household. In addition, many villagers built their houses without following the architectural requirements of Dai traditions (Zuo & Bao, 2012). Recently, local villagers appealed to receive more income from ticketing, to hold more shares in the company, and to have the right to appoint villagers to monitor admission fee collections (Zuo & Bao, 2012). These tensions and conflicts could be attributed to the local villagers' limited participation in the decision-making and planning of the Dai Garden's development and their limited share in the benefits. Local villagers complain that, as the original land users, they cannot make decisions about land rental negotiations; while the bamboo buildings and courtyards where they have resided for generations are forced to open to visitors, they cannot share in the ticket income with the company (Zuo & Bao, 2012).

The Hongcun village case

Hongcun village has a history of more than 880 years, an area of 19.11 ha, and a population of more than 1200 villagers (about 400 households). It is located in the northwest of the Yellow Mountain in Anhui Province. In terms of administrative affiliation, Hongcun village is under Hongcun Township, Yixian County, Huangshan City (a prefecture-level city).[2] It was listed as a UNESCO World Heritage site together with Xidi in 2000, under the name of *Ancient Villages in Southern Anhui – Xidi and Hongcun*. Xidi and Hongcun are two traditional villages with merchant activities as their primary source of income, and family- and clan-based social organisation, and are well known for their regional culture. The overall layout, landscape, architectural form, decoration and construction techniques in Hongcun all maintain the original features of Anhui villages between the 14th and 20th centuries. These historical and cultural features construct Hongcun's core attractions to tourists. It is worth noting that Hongcun is also the place where many scenes of the Oscar-winning film *Crouching Tiger, Hidden Dragon* were produced. Starting in 1986, tourism development in Hongcun experienced three stages: 1986–1994, 1994–1997, and from 1998 to the present, each stage featuring differing community participation characteristics (Jiang *et al.*, 2009; Lu *et al.*, 2010; Xu *et al.*, 2010; Ying & Zhou, 2007; Yu *et al.*, 2013).

During the early stages of the 1986–1988 period, tourism development was initiated by the Tourism Bureau of Yixian County, with just two viewing spots open to tourists with a ticket price of only 4 cents (RMB). At that time, no payment was given to the locals and the potential for tourism had not been recognised by the community (Lu *et al.*, 2010; Yu *et al.*, 2013). From 1994, local people began to recognise the potential value of the village for tourism development. The Villagers' Committee submitted several reports to the township and county governments to initiate village-directed tourism development programmes; however, these requests were not approved (Ying & Zhou, 2007; Yu *et al.*, 2013). In 1996, the Villagers' Committee of Hongcun again made such a request. Eventually, the responsibility of developing tourism at Hongcun was delegated to the township government, and a township government-owned tourism corporation, Hongcun Tourism Development Corporation, was established in June 1996. However, the government effort was not appreciated by the villagers. The Hongcun Villagers' Committee attempted to wrest the rights for tourism operation away from the township government through a contract. In January 1997, the Villager's Committee founded a community-owned tourism corporation, the Hongcun Tourism Service Corporation, and appointed a general manager from among the villagers. However, this community-owned tourism corporation did not succeed in bringing in more visitors and tourism income, especially when benchmarked against the neighbouring Xidi village (Lu *et al.*, 2010; Ying & Zhou, 2007; Yu *et al.*, 2013). There are two reasons for this: (1) Hongcun had poorer road conditions and a lower level of competitiveness in its core tourist attractions than Xidi (Ying & Zhou, 2007); and (2) the Villagers' Committee of Hongcun was less experienced in tourism development and management (Yu *et al.*, 2013).

In 1997, the government of Yixian County signed a contract with a Beijing-based company, Zhongkun Group, and transferred the rights for tourism development in Hongcun to this company for 30 years from January 1998 (Gong, 2012). The contract was signed without informing the Hongcun villagers (Gong, 2012; Lu *et al.*, 2010). Following the contract, a new company called the Jingyi Tourism Development Company (Jingyi Company, hereafter), based on the partnership between the Beijing-based company (*Jing*) and the Yixian County (*yi*), was founded to take charge of tourism development and management issues at Hongcun. In 1998, the new company replaced the onsite tour guides who were villagers, with new non-local recruits (Ying & Zhou, 2007). Local villagers became agitated about the benefit allocation arrangement formulated in 1997 by the Zhongkun Company and the county government without the involvement of the villagers (Gong, 2012; Lu *et al.*, 2010). According to the arrangement, on a yearly basis, Jingyi Company would give: (1) a fixed amount of 170,000 RMB (that is the annual ticket income of 1997) to the village (Gong, 2012; Ying & Zhou, 2007); and (2) 4% of the ticket income to the local township government and 1% of the ticket income to the village (Ying & Zhou, 2007). Eventually, Hongcun village tourism development entered a stage that witnessed the dominating role of an external enterprise. This also marked the beginning of numerous rounds of negotiation between the local government, the Jingyi Company and Hongcun village.

In November 2000, around 300 villagers gathered together and later submitted a report to the county government, requesting that the tourism operation rights be handed back to the villagers. The county government dismissed such a request, claiming that the right of tourism development should be separated from the community's ownership of the heritage architecture and should belong to the government (Ying & Zhou, 2007; Yu *et al.*, 2013). In September 2001, after a failed appeal to the Court of Huangshan City, around 730 villagers (over 60% of the local population) signed an appeal to the Anhui Provincial Court, arguing that the county government infringed their rights of developing tourism in their own village. This appeal, however, was not successful either (Ying & Zhou, 2007; Yu *et al.*, 2013).

In 2002, after several rounds of negotiations, a new agreement on tourism revenue allocation was achieved among the main stakeholders. Under such an agreement, the Jingyi Company takes 67% of the ticket income, the county government 20%, the township government 5%, and the community 8% (Gong, 2012; Lu *et al.*, 2010; Ying & Zhou, 2007; Yu *et al.*, 2013). Although this arrangement was not considered satisfactory by all the villagers, there have been no substantial changes regarding the tourism revenue allocation since 2002 (Ying & Zhou, 2007; Yu *et al.*, 2013).

In addition to the above-mentioned benefits, local villagers can participate in tourism development and gain benefits in the following ways. First, families whose houses are chosen and rented by the Jingyi Company as designated tourist attraction spots covered in the admission ticket can receive a rent varying from 10,000 to 20,000 RMB (Xu *et al.*, 2010), depending on the size and location of the house. Villagers can also get income by renting out their houses to other external business operators. As Xu *et al.* (2010) noted, among the 94 shops along the typical group tour itinerary, over half of them are leased to and operated by external investors who pay the house owners 6000–30,000 RMB in annual rent. Jiang *et al.*'s (2009) study indicated that 93 households (21% of the total) in the village rented out either their houses (40 households) or stalls (53 households). Secondly, villagers can use their own houses and stalls to run businesses like homestays, restaurants and souvenir shops. As shown by Jiang *et al.* (2009), 180 households (42% of the total) operated homestays, stalls and restaurants. In terms of tourism-related income other than the ticket revenue shares, according to Jiang *et al.* (2009), data from the Villagers' Committee of Hongcun indicated that 75% of the total population received an annual income varying from 5000 RMB to 30,000 RMB in relation to tourism.

In spite of the gradual increase in local villagers' income from tourism, conflicts and villager dissatisfaction with benefit sharing are commonly seen in Hongcun; this occurs under the circumstances of an external company dominating tourism development. After 2002 when the latest tourism revenue allocation scheme started, in addition to action requesting tourism development rights and more ticket share, local villagers expressed their dissatisfaction in many ways. It is believed that villagers were disgruntled mainly because they were excluded from the decision-making processes of the village's tourism development (Lu *et al.*, 2010; Wang *et al.*, 2006).

The case of the Daizu Garden illustrates one scenario in Li *et al.*'s (2007: 123) typology, in which, only some community members can share economic benefits from jobs related to the TDP. The Hongcun village case, however, illustrates a different scenario under the same model, in which all community members can share, to some extent, the economic benefits of tourism but still cannot join in the decision-making in the development process.

Limited Participation in Community-dominated Development

In cases of tourism development directed or controlled substantially by the Villagers' Committee, local villagers' participation in tourism development can still be limited; the participation appears to be no more than benefit sharing. It is worth noting that by Chinese law a villagers' committee is elected by villagers and thereby is supposed to represent local community interests. Xidi village in Yixian County, Huangshan City, Anhui Province (Yan & Zhang, 2008; Zhang & Bao, 2009; Zhang *et al.*, 2008) is a representative case illustrating this community participation model.

The Xidi village case

Xidi village is located in the southeast of Yixian County, Anhui Province. It has a history of more than 960 years, an area of 12.96 ha, and a population of more than 1000 villagers (about 300 households). In terms of administrative affiliation, Xidi village falls under Xidi Town, Yixian County, Huangshan City. It was listed as a UNESCO World Heritage site together with Hongcun in 2000. Similarly to Hongcun, the major tourist attractions in Xidi are in its history and culture, for instance, the appearance and layout of non-urban settlements, the historic architecture and decorations in *Hui*('徽') style buildings, traditional *Hui* culture and customs, and the atmosphere of an ancient and traditional village. Xidi started its tourism development early in 1986, when it began to sell tickets to visitors (Zhang & Bao, 2009; Zhang *et al.*, 2008). After a period of initial development and some success, villagers started to consider a better mechanism to control their tourism business. In 1994, a community-owned company, the Xidi Tourism Service Company (the Xidi Company), was founded by the Villagers' Committee of Xidi. The company took full responsibility for tourism development and management in the village. Several attempts were made by the Tourism Bureau of Yixian County to intervene and take over Xidi's tourism development, but all were rejected by the local community.

As the Xidi Company is owned by the Villagers' Committee, the economic benefits brought by tourism development to the villagers in Xidi are more prominent. Ticket sale income is shared by the whole village. The ticket income allocation scheme has been redrawn many times (Yan & Zhang, 2008; Ying & Zhou, 2007; Zhang & Bao, 2009). Currently it works as follows: the total ticket income of the company, after the deductions of relevant taxes and contributions to the Cultural Protection Fund stipulated by Yixian County (20% of the total ticket-sale income), is divided into two equal parts for the Xidi Company and the village. Among the share to the village, 80% is distributed among the villagers, and the rest (20%) is allocated to the village's collective public welfare fund. In addition to sharing the ticket income, Xidi villagers can also benefit from tourism development in other ways. Some villagers run small family-owned tourism businesses, such as homestays, restaurants and souvenir shops. According to Jiang et al. (2009), 47% of the households in Xidi ran homestays, restaurants and souvenir shops. Furthermore, villagers have the opportunity to take jobs with the Xidi Company as tour guides or managers. Since the Xidi Company is a community-owned business, its management is composed of village leaders (Ying & Zhou, 2007; Zhang & Bao, 2009).

Although local villagers in Xidi have a high-level participation in tourism benefit sharing (Jiang et al., 2009; Ying & Zhou, 2007; Zhang & Bao, 2009), they seem to have little involvement in the planning and decision-making of the village's tourism development. This is mostly due to the imbalance of power between the Villagers' Committee elites and ordinary villagers. The former, consisting of local intellectual elites, political elites and business elites (Zhang & Bao, 2009), have obvious advantages in terms of political power over the latter. These elites, commonly seen in village societies in China, play a dominant role in most village affairs, including those relating to tourism development. As China lacks the tradition of a civil society (Lin, 1936: 164), civil awareness or consciousness may still be low among villagers in rural areas. This low level of civil awareness may partly explain the low level of participation of villages in decision-making. In the case of Xidi, as noted in some studies (Xu et al., 2010; Ying & Zhou, 2007; Zhang & Bao, 2009), the lack of an effective democratic decision-making system and dependence on elite governance may have reduced the success of the village's tourism business. To sum up, in the case of Xidi, although tourism development is controlled by the Villagers' Committee, the local community's participation in tourism development is mostly limited to benefit sharing.

As mentioned previously, Li *et al.*'s (2007: 123) typology identifies five community participation scenarios. Accordingly, the case of Xidi village illustrates both *scenario 3* and *scenario 4* in the typology. Specifically, all community members of Xidi can share, to some extent, the economic benefits of tourism, but they cannot exert real influence on the development process (illustrating *scenario 4*). In addition, some of the community members of Xidi (the committee members) may go beyond the stage of benefit sharing to play more active roles, including decision-making, planning and management; however, the chance for such participation is either rare or hard for all community members to secure (illustrating *scenario 3*).

Full Participation in Community-dominated Development

When the local community plays a dominant role in tourism development, it is possible that villagers can fully participate in decision-making and benefit sharing. Yubeng village in Diqing Tibetan Autonomous Prefecture, Yunnan Province (see Guo, 2010; Guo & Huang, 2011; Zhang, 2011) and Langde village in Leishan County, Qiandongnan Prefecture, Guizhou Province (see Chen & Kuang, 2009; Chen *et al.*, 2013; Wang, 2013) represent the model of full community participation in community-dominated development.

The Yubeng village case

Yubeng is a Tibetan village known for its reputation as 'the real Shangri-La'. It is located in Deqing County in Yunnan Province, a remote place with no easy road access. The village has an upper part (Upper Yubeng) and a lower part (Lower Yubeng). Before 2000, most children in the village could not attend elementary school and were not able to speak Mandarin. In 2008, the village had a population of 168 with 34 households. After the mid-1990s, Yubeng became a famous destination for domestic and international backpackers, adventurers and cultural tourists.

The local community has followed a tourism participation model which is labelled as the 'alternate system' by many tourism scholars (e.g. Bao & Sun, 2008; Guo, 2010; Guo & Huang, 2011; Zhang, 2011). This system highlights two basic aspects: horse renting and homestay accommodation. According to Zhang (2011), the alternate system was introduced around 1998 to regulate the rapidly growing horse-renting business in the village's tourism development (Bao & Sun, 2008; Guo & Huang, 2011). Under this system, the

34 households, each owning two or three horses, could select two horses at a time to form the village's horse team. The horses that are used for tourist renting are given a number. The deputy village heads of Upper Yubeng and Lower Yubeng serve as two leaders for the horse teams and are responsible for jointly deciding which horse will be chosen for rental by balloting. Each household should send one person or hire an outsider to work as a groom in the village's collective horse-renting business. Homestay accommodation is another major tourism business in Yubeng village. In this business area, the alternate system works as follows (Bao & Sun, 2008; Guo & Huang, 2011; Zhang, 2011): the 34 households are divided into eight groups, each group consisting of four or five households. These groups work in rotation to accommodate overnight tourists. If tourists choose to stay with households in the rotation, income will be divided equally among the four or five households; if not, then 5 RMB (25% of the average bed rate) from each guest should be given to the household in the shift of rotation by households that received guests but were not in the rotation.

It is worth noting that the introduction and evolution of such an alternate system were collectively decided by the villagers themselves through many rounds of negotiation, derived by the Tibetan beliefs of equality, peace and non-confrontation. What is more important, the local governments at township and county levels have not, at least to date, intervened in the tourism development in terms of daily operation, benefit sharing and decision-making. No external enterprise has been involved in the village tourism.

According to Timothy (1999: 372), benefit sharing and decision-making are two essential aspects of community participation in tourism development. Yubeng village's participation in tourism development has been sufficient and balanced in both aspects. Some researchers (Bao & Sun, 2008; Guo & Huang, 2011; Zhang, 2011) have argued that, the Yubeng village case has realised empowerment to the community in the four aspects as prescribed by Scheyvens (1999), namely economic, psychological, political and social. However, the alternate system in Yubeng village may be vulnerable to external forces, especially when facing apparently more powerful local governments. This alternate system was established and practised by the villagers, without clear reference to China's relevant legislation frameworks, especially those pertaining to property rights and land rights. Therefore, the institutional empowerment is still to be realised (Bao & Sun, 2008).

The Langde village case

Langde is an ethnic Miao community village located in the northwest of Leishan County, Qiandongnan Prefecture, Guizhou Province. Langde village is divided into Upper Langde and Lower Langde, with the former having a population of 540 in 134 households in 2009. Upper Langde village has been studied by a number of scholars and has therefore been well-documented in the literature (e.g. Chen *et al.*, 2013; Chen & Kuang, 2009; Wang, 2013). We hereby only refer to Upper Langde village (Langde village, hereafter) in presenting this case study. Tourism development in Langde village started as early as 1987 (Wang, 2013). Over the years, Langde village has attracted numerous tourists from home and abroad with its beautiful natural environment, colourful ethnic culture and long history (Chen & Kuang, 2009; Chen *et al.*, 2013).

Local villagers participate in tourism development in a variety of ways (Chen *et al.*, 2013; Wang, 2013). First, a Tourist Reception Team (TRT) is established by the Villagers' Committee. The TRT consists of about 20 villagers. Their membership in the TRT is recommended and elected by the villagers. The membership is also rotational. The TRT members are given specific duties in tourism development, such as dealing with external travel agents, organising cultural and dance performances, and maintaining sanitation. Secondly, Miao ethnic dance is a participatory activity that almost every villager can participate in and it is also one of the major tourist attractions in this village. In order to create an ethnic atmosphere and encourage local villagers' participation, the TRT has initiated a scheme referred to by some tourism and ethnology scholars as the 'work-point system' (Chen *et al.*, 2013; Wang, 2013). The distribution of the participatory dance-related income is based on the work-points each family earns. Participants earn varying work-points in accordance to their duties, roles and costumes. For instance, the dance team leader earns 22 points, the TRT members 18 points, male dancers 22 points and female dancers 20 points. To manage the whole process, scorecards with differing work-points are allocated to participating villagers in different stages of the dance. When the dance is over, participating villagers return the cards to the village's accountant who will then calculate each family's total work-points and corresponding share of the income. The value of each work-point is simply calculated through dividing the total income by the total work-points. Twenty-five percent of the collective income from dance performance is reallocated into the village's tourism development fund, which can be used for building infrastructure, maintaining performing venues and instruments, and so on (Chen *et al.*, 2013). Thirdly, according to two village-level policy documents jointly formulated by the TRT and the Villagers' Committee, venues for selling souvenirs are arranged uniformly and a lottery draw is arranged to decide who can sell souvenirs in the given booths. However, the souvenir sellers can only run their businesses after fulfilling dance performance obligations. No fake and shoddy goods may be sold. As the TRT is elected from villagers and the membership is rotational, it enables a better representation of the villagers in the decision-making process. In such a case, villagers are involved in both the benefit sharing and the decision-making of tourism development, thus making it a relatively more inclusive participation practice in tourism development.

According to Li *et al.*'s (2007: 123) typology, the cases of Yubeng village and Langde village illustrate *scenario 5* in the typology, in which all community members of the two villages can get involved in the entire TDP (both benefit sharing and decision-making) as legitimate stakeholders.

Current State of Community Participation in the TDP in China

Generally speaking, community participation in tourism development in China is not up to standard (e.g. Bao & Sun, 2006; Bao & Zuo, 2012; Luo, 2006; Sun, 2008; Yang & Cen, 2013; Zhou *et al.*, 2009; Zuo, 2013; Zuo & Bao, 2012) as prescribed by international scholars (e.g. Scheyvens, 1999; Timothy, 1999), except for a few relatively successful cases, such as Yubeng village (Bao & Sun, 2008; Guo & Huang, 2011; Zhang, 2011) and Langde village (Chen *et al.*, 2013; Wang, 2013). Limitations to community participation in tourism development in China, as recorded in the extant Chinese literature, could be summarised into the following three aspects. First, lack of endogenous development capacity of the local community has been commonly identified as an obstacle to the realisation of community participation in tourism development, especially in relation to decision-making (e.g. Bao & Sun, 2006; Luo, 2006; Sun, 2008; Zuo, 2013). Endogenous capacity here refers to all the necessary production factors, such as capital, technology, information, management, personal skills and knowledge and civil rights awareness among community members.

Secondly, the inappropriate role played by the government in institutional arrangements has been another commonly identified limitation in realising community participation in tourism development. There are many issues involved in this aspect, including the pro-growth mentality in national governance which ignores the basic rights and interests of local communities (e.g. Luo, 2006; Rao, 2013; Zuo, 2013), and land property rights policies ignoring the rights of local communities in tourism development (e.g. Bao & Sun, 2006; Bao & Zuo, 2012; Luo, 2006; Zuo & Bao, 2012). Thirdly, the imbalance of power relations among major tourism stakeholders has been identified as key to understanding the current situations of community participation in tourism development in China. The imbalance of power relations is caused by many factors. The divergent capacities among different stakeholders and the current political institutions are regarded as major causes, among others (e.g. Bao & Sun, 2006; Weng & Peng, 2010).

Conclusion

This chapter first establishes a matrix of models of community participation in tourism, by using the dominant stakeholder and the depth (types) of local communities' participation as key dimensions (see Figure 4.1). Following this matrix, four models are identified as existent in China and are elaborated with cases illuminating their characteristics. As many cases in this chapter show, when local governments and/or external investors control the decision-making process of tourism development, local residents are mostly able to participate in benefit sharing; however, in most cases, community participation in decision-making is not in place. As the Yubeng and Langde cases indicate, only when tourism development is fully under the control of the local community and the Villagers' Committee really represents the whole village's interests, can a complete practice of community participation in tourism development in terms of both benefit sharing and decision-making (Timothy, 1999: 372) be achieved. When the Villagers' Committee does not stand for the interests of the entire village but for that of a few elites, even where the Villagers' Committee controls tourism development, ordinary villagers cannot fully participate in decision-making and benefit sharing. This has been demonstrated in many cases in China, like the Xidi case reported in this chapter.

Undoubtedly, benefit sharing and decision-making are not independent processes or stages in community participation in tourism development; on the contrary, they should be interconnected and overlap each other. In developing countries like China, where tourism is the only or the major source of income for many rural/ethnic communities, guaranteeing the community's economic benefits from tourism development should be and always has been a priority to the major stakeholders involved, namely local authorities, external investors and the local community. However, only when local villagers can participate in the decision-making process can they decide the future of tourism development in their community and the future of their own lives. Therefore, benefit sharing should be better viewed as a foundation and decision-making viewed as a guarantee in local community participation in tourism development in China.

Notes

(1) According to the *Organic Law of the Villagers' Committees* in China, a villagers' committee is an autonomous organisation elected by the villagers within the whole administrative village ('行政村'). A Communist Party committee is also established at the administrative village level. An administrative village is administrative unit which is self-governed by a villagers' committee; a natural village ('自然村') is usually a rural settlement. In terms of both geography and administration, an administrative village is usually constituted of many natural villages.

(2) The Constitution of PRC designates three levels of government in China: province level (including autonomous region, municipality and special administrative region); county level (including county-level city, autonomous county and district under prefecture-level city); and township level (including sub-district, town and district under county-level city). However, there could be a prefecture level (including prefectural-level city, autonomous prefecture, sub-provincial-level city) government between province and county in place.

References

Bahaire, T. and Elliott-White, M. (1999) Community participation in tourism planning and development in the historic city of York, England. *Current Issues in Tourism* 2 (3), 243–76.

Bao, J. and Sun, J. (2006) A contrastive study on the difference in community participation in tourism between China and the West. *Acta Geographica Sinica* 61 (4), 401–413.

Bao, J. and Sun, J. (2008) Community participation in tourism of Yubeng Village: Means of participation and its significance for empowerment. *Tourism Forum* 1 (1), 58–65.

Bao, J. and Zuo, B. (2012) Legislating for tourist attractions rights. *Tourism Tribune* 27 (7), 11–18.

Bramwell, B. and Sharman, A. (2000) Approaches to sustainable tourism planning and community participation: The case of the Hope Valley. In R. Greg and D. Hall (eds) *Tourism and Sustainable Community Development* (pp. 17–35). London: Routledge.

Cao, Z. (2011) The vertically decentralized authoritarianism and the mechanisms of political stability in China. *Sociological Studies* 25 (1), 1–40.

Chen, Z. and Kuang, Z. (2009) The dilemma of individual rationality and collective activity in the community-leading tourism development model of the Langde Miao Ethnic Village. *Academic Exploration* 3, 72–79.

Chen, Z., Li, L. and Li, T. (2013) The organizational evolution, systematic construction and empowerment significance of Langde Miao's community tourism. *Tourism Tribune* 28 (6), 75–86.

Gong, S. (2012) The study of the interests of formers maximize business model in Wannan (Southern Anhui) rural tourism: Based on the examples of Xidi and Hongcun. Masters degree thesis, Anhui University, Hefei, China.

Guo, W. (2010) Study on the 'alternate system' mode regarding rural residents' participation in tourism development and community empowerment effectiveness. *Tourism Tribune* 25 (3), 76–83.

Guo, W. and Huang, Z. (2011) Study on the development of community power and functions under the background of the development of rural tourism: Based on the investigation of two representative cases in Daizu garden and Yubeng community, Yunnan Province. *Tourism Tribune* 26 (12), 83–92.

Hung, K., Sirakaya-Turk, E. and Ingram, L.J. (2011) Testing the efficacy of an integrative model for community participation. *Journal of Travel Research* 50 (3), 276–288.

Jiang, H., Wang, Y. and Li, J. (2009) Research on development models of ancient villages based on community management: A case study of World Cultural Heritage-Xidi Village and Hongcun Village. *East China Economic Management* 23 (8), 24–28.

Li, W. (2006) Community decision-making: Participation in development. *Annals of Tourism Research* 33, 132–143.

Li, Y. (2004) Exploring community tourism in China: The case of Nanshan Cultural Tourism Zone. *Journal of Sustainable Tourism* 12 (3), 175–193.

Li, Y., Lai, K. and Feng, X. (2007) The problem of 'Guanxi' for actualizing community tourism: A case study of relationship networking in China. *Tourism Geographies: An International Journal of Tourism Space, Place and Environment* 9 (2), 115–138.

Lin, Y. (1936) *My Country and My People*. London: William Heineman.

Liu, J., Wei, Y., Liu, C., Xu, S., Chen, X. and Xiao, Y. (2008) A case study on the model of tourist enterprise-dominant community participation in Nanling National Forest Park. *Tourism Tribune* 23 (6), 80–86.

Lu, S., Chen, S. and Pan, H. (2010) Preliminary study on the assessment of tourism sustainability in an ancient village: Taking World Cultural Heritage Site Hongcun as an example. *Tourism Tribune* 25 (1), 17–25.

Luo, Y. (2006) A study on the assuring mechanism of the interest of community participation in tourism development of ethnic village. *Tourism Tribune* 21 (10), 45–48.

O'Brien, K.J. and Li, L. (2006) *Rightful Resistance in Rural China*. Cambridge: Cambridge University Press.

Rao, Y. (2013) Elite labour immigration and marginalization of local community in tourism development: A case study of Sanya City, China. *Tourism Tribune* 28 (1), 46–53.

Scheyvens, R. (1999) Ecotourism and the empowerment of local community. *Tourism Management* 20 (2), 245–249.

Sofield, T.H.B. and Li, F.M.S. (1998) Tourism development and cultural policies in China. *Annals of Tourism Research* 25 (2), 362–392.

Sofield, T.H.B. and Li, F.M.S. (2011) Tourism governance and sustainable national development in China: A macro-level synthesis. *Journal of Sustainable Tourism* 19 (4–5), 501–534.

Sun, J. (2008) Empowerment theory and the construction of community capability in the development of tourism. *Tourism Tribune* 23 (9), 22–27.

Timothy, D.J. (1999) Participatory planning: A view of tourism in Indonesia. *Annals of Tourism Research* 26 (2), 371–391.

Tosun, C. (1999) Towards a typology of community participation in the tourism development process. *Anatolia: An International Journal of Tourism and Hospitality Research* 10 (2), 113–134.

Tosun, C. (2000) Limits to community participation in the tourism development process in developing countries. *Tourism Management* 21 (6), 613–633.

Tosun, C. (2006) Expected nature of community participation in tourism development. *Tourism Management* 27 (3), 493–504.

Walder, A.G. (1995) Local governments as industrial firms: An organizational analysis of China's transitional economy. *American Journal of Sociology* 101 (2), 263–301.

Wang. C. (2013) A study of development patterns for minority people's tourism villages. *Journal of Guizhou Minzu University (Philosophy and Social Science)* 6, 61–64.

Wang, C. and Huang, F. (2013) From community involvement to community empowerment: A case study of Kaiping watchtower and villages. *Human Geography* 28 (1), 141–149.

Wang, L., Lu, L., Wang, Y., Yang, Z., Liang, D. and Lu, S. (2006) Study on relationship between tourism stakeholders and impacts of tourism development in ancient village resorts: A case study of World Cultural Heritage Xidi and Hongcun Village. *Resource Development & Market* 22 (3), 276–279.

Weng, S. and Peng, H. (2010) The impact of power relationship on community participation in tourism development: A case from Furong Village at Nanxi River Basin, Zhejiang Province. *Tourism Tribune* 25 (9), 51–57.

Xu, H., Wu, Y. and Peng, L. (2010) Path dependence in travel route formation in ancient village tourism destinations: An empirical study of Xidi and Hongcun. *Geographical Research* 29 (7), 1324–1334.

Yan, Y. and Zhang, L. (2008) A comparative research on mechanism of community participation under different operating modes: examples of ancient-village tourism. *Human Geography* 23 (4), 89–94.

Yang, X. and Cen, Q. (2013) An empirical study of legal practices in community tourism participation in China. *Tourism Tribune* 28 (8), 51–58.

Ying, T. and Zhou, Y. (2007) Community, governments and external capitals in China's rural cultural tourism: A comparative study of two adjacent villages. *Tourism Management* 28 (1), 96–107.

Yu, Y. (2008) An analysis on the community-oriented rural tourism development based on game theory. *Economic Geography* 28 (3), 519–522.

Yu, R., Liang, L., Li, D., Zhu, H. and Zhu, S. (2013) Tourism population invasion, succession and the spatial order recombination of ancient village – a case study of Hongcun Village. *Economic Geography* 33 (8), 165–170.

Zhang, J. (2008) *Marketization and Democracy in China*. New York: Routledge.

Zhang, W. (2010) *The Logic of the Market*. Shanghai: Shanghai People's Press.

Zhang, X. (2011) Tourism and villagers without 'history': Based on the rethinking of the study of Yubeng Village. *Tourism Tribune* 26 (3), 62–69.

Zhang, X. and Bao, J. (2009) Tourism development and rural vicissitudes: The hypothesis of 'origin-dynamics'. *Tourism Tribune* 24 (6), 19–24.

Zhang, X., Ding, P. and Bao, J. (2008) Income distribution, tourist commercialisation, and Hukou status: A socioeconomic analysis of tourism in Xidi, China. *Current Issues in Tourism* 11 (6), 549–566.

Zhou, F. (2006) A decade of tax-sharing: The system and its evolution. *Social Sciences in China* 6, 100–115.

Zhou, Y., Jiang, J. and Wang, X. (2009) A study of community-driven endogenous rural tourism development model. *Tourism Science* 23 (4), 36–41.

Zuo, B. (2013) Encompassing interest: Interest coordination of community involving pattern of tourism development. *Tourism Science* 27 (1), 1–14.

Zuo, B. and Bao, J. (2012) Institutional empowerment: Community participation and changes of land property rights in tourism development. *Tourism Tribune* 27 (2), 23–31.

5 Tourist Market and Behaviour Studies: The Chinese Foci

Introduction

The Chinese tourism research community has paid more attention to tourism supply issues than to the demand-side issues. Demand-side tourism research in China is still underdeveloped compared to research from the international tourism community. However, it is interesting to see what focused areas Chinese tourism researchers have been working on and what academic contributions they have made. In this chapter, tourist market studies and behaviour studies are critically reviewed independently, as the terms of *tourist market* and *tourist behaviour* in Chinese bear somewhat different connotations and therefore are two slightly different areas of knowledge. In the following sections, an overview of tourist market studies, their major focuses and methods is provided. After an overview of the publications and methods used, the progress made in each of the major topic areas of tourist behaviour studies is discussed. Finally, the academic contributions to Chinese tourist market and tourist behaviour research are examined.

Tourist Market Studies: An Overview

As shown in Table 5.1, between 2006 and 2013 62 research articles from the four leading Chinese tourism journals (*Tourism Tribune, Tourism Science, Economic Geography* and *Human Geography*) can be identified as being related to the tourist market. The most frequent topic was 'market profiles and segmentation' (45.2%), followed by 'source market structure (temporal and spatial)' (35.5%), while articles on 'market size and its changes' and 'market policy and marketing strategies' only accounted for 9.7% and 6.5%,

Table 5.1 Thematic categorisation of tourist market-related articles published in four Chinese journals, 2006–2013

	Tourism Tribune	Tourism Science	Human Geography	Economic Geography	Total
Source market structure (temporal and spatial)	6	3	4	9	22
Market profiles and segmentation	18	2	3	5	28
Market size and its changes	1	1	1	3	6
Market policy and marketing strategies	3	1	0	0	4
Others	2	0	0	0	2
Total	30	7	8	17	62

respectively. Specifically, in terms of publication distribution among the four journals, two geographical journals, namely *Economic Geography* (40.9%) and *Human Geography* (18.1%), together published 60% of articles on 'source market structure (temporal and spatial)', while *Tourism Tribune* published most of the studies on 'market profiles and segmentation' (64.3%). In terms of research themes, the majority of the existing articles (85%) on 'source market structure (temporal and spatial)' focused on the inbound/international source markets.

As shown in Table 5.2, most of the published tourist market research adopted quantitative methods. Papers with first-hand data sources (43.5%) and second-hand data sources (35.5%) accounted for 79% of all those published in the eight-year period; there were 13 published articles (21%) under the category of 'descriptive presentation without methods'. Notably, most of the quantitative articles using second-hand data sources were dedicated to analysing the temporal and spatial structures of the inbound/international source markets, employing diversified methods and indicators such as the shift-share method (SSM; e.g. Jin *et al.*, 2010; Quan *et al.*, 2012), the preference scale and competition state (e.g. Liu & Gao, 2007; Zhang & Gao, 2007), the tourist concentration index (e.g. Ji & Chen, 2013; Tao & Huang, 2012), and the importance-performance analysis (IPA; e.g. Ji & Chen, 2013). Accordingly, most of the quantitative research with first-hand data sources adopted questionnaire surveys in order to understand the profiles and segmentations/classifications of specific markets, such as international markets (Xu, 2008), rural tourism markets in peri-urban areas (Su & Wang, 2007), and the domestic leisure and holiday markets (Wang, 2006), among others.

Table 5.2 Method categorisation of tourist market-related articles published in four Chinese journals, 2006–2013

	Tourism Tribune	Tourism Science	Human Geography	Economic Geography	Total
First-hand data and statistical analysis	9	4	4	10	27
Second-hand data and statistical analysis	14	0	3	5	22
Descriptive presentation without methods	7	3	1	2	13
Total	30	7	8	17	62

Tourist Behaviour Studies: The Chinese Foci

Overview

As indicated in Table 5.3, between 2006 and 2013 a total of 208 papers from the four Chinese journals were identified as relating to tourist behaviours. The most frequently covered topic was 'tourist perceptions/cognition' (25.5%), followed by 'behavioural intention' (18.8%) and 'satisfaction' (14.4%). Articles on the topics of 'needs, motivations and expectations' and 'decision-making/destination choice' accounted for 10.6% and 6.7% of all those published, respectively. Of these articles, 3.8% can be categorised as 'sub-regional spatial behaviours' studies. Although topics such as 'perceived benefits of travel and tourism' and 'interaction among tourists' have emerged as research areas in the international tourism academic community as reflected in mainstream English tourism journals (e.g. Chen & Petrick, 2013; Chen et al., 2014; Durko & Petrick, 2013), articles on these topics in Chinese journals are still rare and sporadic.

With regard to research method, six different types were identified among the articles. Twenty-four published articles (11.5%) either did not clearly state the methods or only used simple statistics such as percentage, mean, and frequency in their main body discussion. Such articles can hardly be treated as research papers as they don't seem to post clearly defined research questions, and they cannot be regarded as conceptual research or basic research either. According to Xin et al. (2013: 84), conceptual research is 'a set of activities that focus on the systematic analysis and profound understanding of tourism concepts'. Basic research 'is executed without thought of a practical end goal, without specific applications or products in

Table 5.3 Thematic categorisation of tourist behaviour-related articles published in four Chinese journals, 2006–2013

	Tourism Tribune	Tourism Science	Human Geography	Economic Geography	Total
Cross-cultural comparison of tourist behaviours	3	3	0	0	6
Satisfaction[a]	19	2	6	3	30
Tourist perceptions/cognition	21	15	11	6	53
Needs, motivations and expectations	12	7	2	1	22
Behavioural intention	22	10	4	3	39
Perceived benefits of travel and tourism	2	0	0	0	2
Interaction among tourists	2	0	1	0	3
Tourist power and rights	2	0	0	0	2
Dining and shopping behaviours	2	1	3	0	6
Decision-making/destination choice	5	4	2	3	14
Sub-regional spatial behaviours	6	1	1	0	8
Sense of place/place attachment	0	0	5	1	6
Others	6	4	4	3	17
Total	102	47	39	20	208

Notes: [a]'Satisfaction' here represents studies that specialise in the evaluation, measurement and influencing factors of tourist satisfaction, while those using 'satisfaction' as a mediator are categorised as 'behavioural intention' studies.

mind' (National Science Foundation, 1953: 38) and therefore lays the foundation for knowledge advancement that leads on to applied output later, occasionally as a result of unexpected discoveries. Following these definitions, conceptual research and basic research can be found in a small proportion (6.2%) of the tourist behaviour studies. Major concepts discussed in such studies include tourist power (Lv *et al.*, 2011), satisfaction equilibrium (Chen *et al.*, 2013), and tourist perception and cognition (Bai *et al.*, 2008).

Many studies applied sophisticated statistical methods including regression analysis, factor analysis and path analysis. In 25% of the articles structural equation modelling (SEM) was adopted as the methodology, reconfirming the increasing use and popularity of the SEM in tourist behaviour studies in China (Gao *et al.*, 2012; Xie & Yu, 2010). Meanwhile, papers using sophisticated statistical methods other than SEM accounted for 48.1% of all those published; among different non-SEM methods, regression analysis, factor analysis and cluster analysis were widely used.

The number of studies applying mixed methods (both quantitative and qualitative) has recently risen slightly among the tourism research community in China. Articles using mixed methods represented 7.2% of all the published tourist behaviour articles over the eight-year period. Many articles stated that both quantitative and qualitative methods were used; however, upon close examination, these studies only briefly mentioned that qualitative methods, such as web-based content analysis and interviews, had been used to develop and refine the survey questionnaires. The detailed process of such qualitative research was seldom reported, therefore making the claimed qualitative research component less supported. On the other hand, very few studies were found to apply well-prescribed qualitative research design.

Tourist perceptions/cognition

Chinese scholars investigated a variety of topics in the field of tourist perceptions and cognition between 2006 and 2013. Frequently researched topics include tourist interests/attractiveness perception (e.g. Liu *et al.*, 2008; Song *et al.*, 2006), tourism service quality perception (e.g. Li & Gan, 2011; Yao *et al.*, 2008), perceived value (e.g. Huang & Huang, 2007; Li & Zhang, 2010), perception of authenticity in ethnic and cultural/heritage tourism settings (e.g. Gao & Zheng, 2010; Lin & Hu, 2013), destination safety and risk perception (e.g. Chiu *et al.*, 2011; Zou & Zheng, 2012), destination image perception and cognition (e.g. Xie *et al.*, 2010; Zhang & Ma, 2007), spatial perception (e.g. Pan, 2009; Zhao *et al.*, 2013), and transport/accessibility perception (e.g. Lu *et al.*, 2011; Wang *et al.*, 2010).

It should be noted that destination image, representing the totality of beliefs, conceptions, feelings and expectations that tourists hold toward a specific place (Pearce, 2005), is associated with tourist decision-making/destination choice and is therefore an important behavioural construct for destination marketers. Tourism academics in China have examined a variety of interesting topics in relation to destination image. For instance, Feng (2011) conducted an analysis of multidimensional discourse on the blogs of Chinese and Western tourists to understand Beijing's destination image. Gan *et al.* (2013) investigated the destination image of Tibet among domestic Chinese tourists and examined the relationship between the cognitive image, emotional image and overall image. Other studies have also examined the impacts of perceived distance (e.g. Zhang *et al.*, 2006) and cultural differences (Wu *et al.*, 2010) on destination image.

Needs, motivations and expectations

Travel motivation is a fundamental behavioural construct in tourism studies and thus is a basic concept of tourism development. The motivations or reasons behind travel are covert in that they reflect an individual's personal needs, wants and expectations (Gee *et al.*, 1984; Pearce, 2005). Tourist motivations, needs and expectations have formed an important topic area for recent tourist behaviour studies in China. Chinese tourism researchers have examined tourist motivations, needs and expectations in various settings and forms of travel, including the motivations of holidaymakers (Xu, 2007), film-induced tourists (Wu & Hou, 2006), self-drive tourists (Zhang *et al.*, 2006), repeat visitors (Chen & Huang, 2010) and heritage tourists (Dong, 2011); demands and expectations for interpretation in museums (Gan & Lu, 2012; Hong & Tao, 2006), geo-parks (Zhang *et al.*, 2010) and forest parks (Luo *et al.*, 2008). In addition, domestic tourists' motivations for visiting an earthquake-struck destination (Gan *et al.*, 2010), Chinese tourists' expectations for visiting Canada as an outbound destination (Huang, 2008), and the impacts of tourists' motivation on their expectations (Wang & Qu, 2013) and experiences (Fang *et al.*, 2013), have all been investigated.

Decision-making/destination choice

Tourist choice making in selecting a specific destination or product is one of the central topics in tourist behaviour studies. When choosing a destination, tourists make financial and expenditure commitments in multiple service domains (e.g. airlines, hotels); therefore, tourist decision-making is of key interest to destination marketers (Pearce, 2005). As reflected in the articles published between 2006 and 2013, tourism academics in China also examined destination-related decision-making, particularly exploring the factors that influence tourists' decision-making/destination choice. For example, Chen and Huang (2008) identified four factors which influence repeat visitors' decision to revisit a destination, namely the anticipated service quality, anticipated tourist attraction, anticipated value and past experiences. Using logistic regression analysis, Zhang *et al.* (2008) investigated the impacts of tourists' motivations on destination choice (distance). Similarly, Zhao's (2009) study on inbound tourists in Beijing, Shanghai and Guangzhou found that two major factors, namely tourist sociodemographic characteristics (profession, length of stay in China, family structure, travel pattern, travel motivation) and the three different entry-port cities chosen (Beijing,

Shanghai and Guangzhou), affected inbound tourists' decisions about visiting destinations in West China. Some studies developed conceptual models. For instance, Jiao (2006) established a conceptual model of travel decision-making based on tourist preference and risk perception. Yao and Luo (2006) proposed an amended version of the theory of planned behaviour model in the Chinese context.

Satisfaction

In recent years, tourist satisfaction has become a popular topic for tourist behaviour studies in China. In addition to examining satisfaction as a mediator or moderator between some behavioural antecedents and tourists' behavioural intentions, tourism academics in China have also focused on the evaluation and measurement of tourist satisfaction and the identification of key factors determining tourist satisfaction. Different research methods have been applied and these studies can be classified into three basic categories. The first category applies a direct measurement of tourist satisfaction. For instance, Qiu et al. (2013) measured tourist satisfaction with the soundscape in a tourist area in Nanjing, using a 5-point Likert scale with 1 representing 'not satisfied at all' and 5 representing 'very satisfied'. The second category applies the widely used importance-performance analysis (IPA) and its modified forms. The IPA technique has been applied to study the satisfaction of different types of tourists, such as inbound tourists to the Chengdu Research Base of Giant Panda Breeding (Liu et al., 2009a), business travellers in Shanghai (Hu, 2008), and American pleasure tourists visiting China (Wang et al., 2010).

The third category is characterised by some self-developed tourist satisfaction measurement models. The Research Group of China Tourist Satisfaction Index (2012) constructed the tourist satisfaction evaluation system (TSES), which consists of three layers of indicators covering the results of field survey, web comments, tourist complaints and quality monitoring. The TSES was later used and validated in measuring tourist satisfaction in 50 Chinese cities (He, 2011, 2012; Research Group of China Tourist Satisfaction Index, 2012). Similarly, Wang et al. (2011) developed a three-layer tourist satisfaction index measurement model which includes criteria, factors and indicators.

An increasing amount of academic attention has been paid to examining the factors influencing tourist satisfaction in China. These factors include both psychological factors and destination attributes. The former includes tourists' service quality perceptions (e.g. He, 2011, 2012), affect (Luo et al., 2011) and cognitive distance (Zhang et al., 2011b), while the latter covers regional economic development levels, environmental protection, urban greening and richness of tourism attractions (e.g. Luo *et al.*, 2013) and authenticity (Feng & Sha, 2007).

Behavioural intentions

In the recent Chinese tourism literature, tourist behavioural intention has often been operationalised in two different approaches. The first operationalisation approach treats tourist behavioural intention as an implied tourist loyalty construct to the destination, most often directly measured by tourists' intention to revisit the destination (revisit intention) and their intention to recommend the destination to friends, relatives and others (word-of-mouth recommendation). The second approach contextualises behavioural intentions in different situations (e.g. environmental behaviour intention, willingness to participate in the making of movies and TV series in film-based attractions, and willingness to pay for specific products and services). As one of the most frequently researched areas in the study of tourist behaviour in China, behavioural intention has been mostly treated as a consequence of tourists' experiences and destination attributes. In the studies employing the first operationalisation approach, those constructs examined as impacting on behavioural intention (tourist loyalty) include destination personality (e.g. Tang *et al.*, 2011; Zhang & Bai, 2011), destination image (e.g. Bao & Hu, 2008; Liu, 2013), tourism enterprise [corporate] social responsibility (e.g. Shen, 2012; Su & Huang, 2012), tourism service quality (e.g. Xie & Li, 2007; Xie *et al.*, 2007) and service equity (e.g. Su & Huang, 2010; Xie *et al.*, 2007), tourist motivation (e.g. Zhang, 2008, 2012), interactions among tourists (e.g. Jiang & Zhang, 2013), tourist place attachment (e.g. Bai, 2010; Yu *et al.*, 2010), tourist emotional experience (e.g. Bai & Guo, 2010), and tourist personal involvement (e.g. Liu *et al.*, 2009b). In these studies, satisfaction was commonly designated as a mediator between these antecedent constructs and behavioural intentions.

Tourism researchers in China employing the second operationalisation approach have also studied the relationships between tourist environmental attitudes and their environmental behavioural intentions in natural heritage sites (e.g. Qi *et al.*, 2009), tourists' willingness to participate in the making of movies and TV series in film-based attractions (e.g. Guo, 2008), to pay for educational services in tourist areas (e.g. Wen & Wei, 2012), and certificated ecotourism products (e.g. Zhou *et al.*, 2006).

Geographical studies of tourist behaviour

In addition to the above-mentioned tourist behaviour studies from a wide variety of psychological perspectives, tourist behaviour studies conducted by geographers (referred to in this chapter as geographical studies of tourist behaviours) are evident. These geographical studies of tourist behaviours could be classified into two basic categories. The first category refers to studies of tourist behaviours within a relatively small tourist space. In this regard, researchers have examined the spatial and temporal behaviours (mainly movements) of tourists within a tourist area, for instance, the Summer Palace in Beijing (Huang, 2009; Huang & Ma, 2011), and the Gulangyu Islet in Xiamen, Fujian Province (Li et al., 2013). The two Summer Palace studies used data from questionnaire surveys and GPS surveys, respectively, while the Gulangyu Islet study used photos from *Panoramio*, a website affiliated to Google for uploading photos. Some other studies examined tourists' spatial and temporal behaviours within large cities. For instance, Li and Hao (2009) investigated tourists' spatial movements in the city of Xi'an; and Lu (2008) examined tourists' temporal behaviours in the county of Huangzhong, where the famous Kumbum Monastery (also known as the Taer Lamasery in Chinese) is located.

The second category deals with tourists' sense of place. Topics in this category include identifying the spatial characteristics of event-goers' place identity (Dai & Xiao, 2012), understanding the differences of sense of place between tourists and local residents (Qiu et al., 2012), and examining the factors influencing tourists' sense of place (Wang et al., 2013; Xiao et al., 2012; Zhou et al., 2010).

Other tourist behaviour studies

Apart from the above-mentioned topic areas, other behavioural studies were also identified. For example, in the area of cross-cultural comparison, Chinese tourism academics have investigated the perceived value differences between Chinese and Western tourists in cultural heritage settings (Sui et al., 2010), and motivational and environmental attitude differences between Chinese and Western tourists in ecotourism settings (Li & Xie, 2008). Additionally, topics such as tourists' dining behaviour (Luo & Zhang, 2010), shopping behaviour (Bai & Ma, 2007), tourist power (Lv et al., 2011), and tourist rights (Huang & Han, 2010) were also examined. It is worth noting that Chinese researchers have recently looked into the benefits of travel and tourism and the interactions among tourists. Publications related to the former theme include Tan et al.'s (2010) study on the relationships among rural tourists' life pressure perception, leisure coping strategies and health, and Zhao and Wu's (2013) work on the relationship between place identity and the leisure benefits of individual Mainland Chinese visitors to Taiwan. Recent works in the latter theme could be found in Jiang and Hu's (2011) investigation into the categories of tourist-to-tourist interactions using the critical incident technique, Liang's (2009) analysis of the interactions among international tourists and local residents in Xi'an, and Peng's (2013) typology study on the social relationships of tourist-to-tourist interactions.

Tourist Market and Behaviour Studies in China: Reflections on the Academic Contributions

Bao *et al.* (2014) have recently suggested in their critical review that it is time to reveal 'where we are now' in tourism research by Chinese scholars residing in China. Indeed, after more than 30 years of development, the need for a critical review of academic contributions applies not only to tourism research in China as a whole, but also to every single specific topic area, including the area of tourist markets and behaviours. In the following sections, the academic contributions that have been made in tourist market and behaviour studies in China over the eight-year period between 2006 and 2010 are critically evaluated.

Theoretical contributions

There has been two different approaches to defining theory in social sciences. Many scholars define theory in terms of the relationships between independent and dependent variables (e.g. Bacharach, 1989; Campbell, 1990). Other scholars have defined theory in terms of narratives and accounts. For instance, DiMaggio (1995: 391) defined a theory as 'an account of a social process, with emphasis on empirical tests of the plausibility of the narrative as well as careful attention to the scope conditions of the account'. From such a perspective, a theory is mainly evaluated by the richness of its account, the degree to which it provides a close fit to empirical data, and the degree to which it results in novel insight (Colquitt & Zapata-Phelan, 2007; Eisenhardt, 1989). In social sciences research, theory allows scholars to describe and explain a process or sequence of events (DiMaggio, 1995), and even serves as the basic and ultimate goal of scientific research (Kerlinger & Lee, 2000).

Theoretical contributions have long been discussed in management studies (e.g. Colquitt & Zapata-Phelan, 2007; Corley & Gioa, 2011; Whetten, 1989), and recently often debated in consumer research (e.g. Lynch, 2011; Lynch *et al.*, 2012; Park, 2012), which is much closer to the study of tourist behaviour and tourism studies (Chen & Bao, 2011). Generally speaking, the theoretical contributions of empirical research are made along two dimensions: theory building and theory testing (e.g. Colquitt & Zapata-Phelan,

2007; Lynch *et al.*, 2012). Colquitt and Zapata-Phelan (2007) created a typology of theoretical contributions, which reflects the theoretical contributions of empirical research in terms of both theory building and theory testing.

According to Colquitt and Zapata-Phelan's (2007) typology (Figure 5.1), the empirical articles could be divided into five distinct types. Adopting Colquitt and Zapata-Phelan's (2007) typology and computations, we examined the academic contributions of the reviewed tourist market articles (49) (Table 5.2) and the tourist behaviour articles (181) (Table 5.4). However, only 45 of the 181 tourist behaviour articles were subjected to theoretical contribution evaluation, as the rest of them are not theory-driven research and will be treated differently and evaluated separately in the following section. As a result, 33 of the 45 articles were identified as *reporters* (Colquitt & Zapata-Phelan, 2007). *Reporters* are empirical articles that possess relatively low levels of both theory building and theory testing. They receive a rating of 1 or 2 on theory building and a 1 or 2 on theory testing (Figure 5.1). This type of research, in terms of theory building, attempted to examine the effects or relationships that have been the subject of prior theorising (at position 1 in Figure 5.1), or attempted to replicate previously demonstrated effects (at position 2 in Figure 5.1); while in terms of theory testing, they are inductive or grounded predictions (hypotheses) with logical speculation (position 1), or grounded predictions with references to past findings (position 2). For example, Jiang and Zhang (2013) conducted a study to test the effects of tourist-to-tourist interaction on tourists' re-patronage intentions. Their hypotheses were developed with logical speculations and with reference to past findings, while the examined relationships and effects have been subjects of previous theorising in customer interaction literature.

Secondly, 12 of the 45 articles were identified as *qualifiers*. *Qualifiers* are defined as empirical articles that contain moderate levels of both theory testing and theory building (receiving a rating of 2.5–3.5 on both theory testing and theory building; Colquitt & Zapata-Phelan, 2007). For instance, Zhang *et al.*'s (2011a) study of the effects of destination image dimensions on tourist behavioural intentions represents an example of the *qualifier* articles. In this paper, hypotheses were developed and presented with reference to conflicting findings in the destination image literature and some effects found in the non-Chinese context.

Unfortunately, none of the 45 articles could be identified as a study in the more advanced theory-building and theory-testing domains (i.e. the tester, builder and expander positions in Figure 5.1). Specifically, according to Colquitt and Zapata-Phelan (2007), a *tester* is an empirical article that contains high levels of theory testing (receiving a rating of 4 or 5 on theory

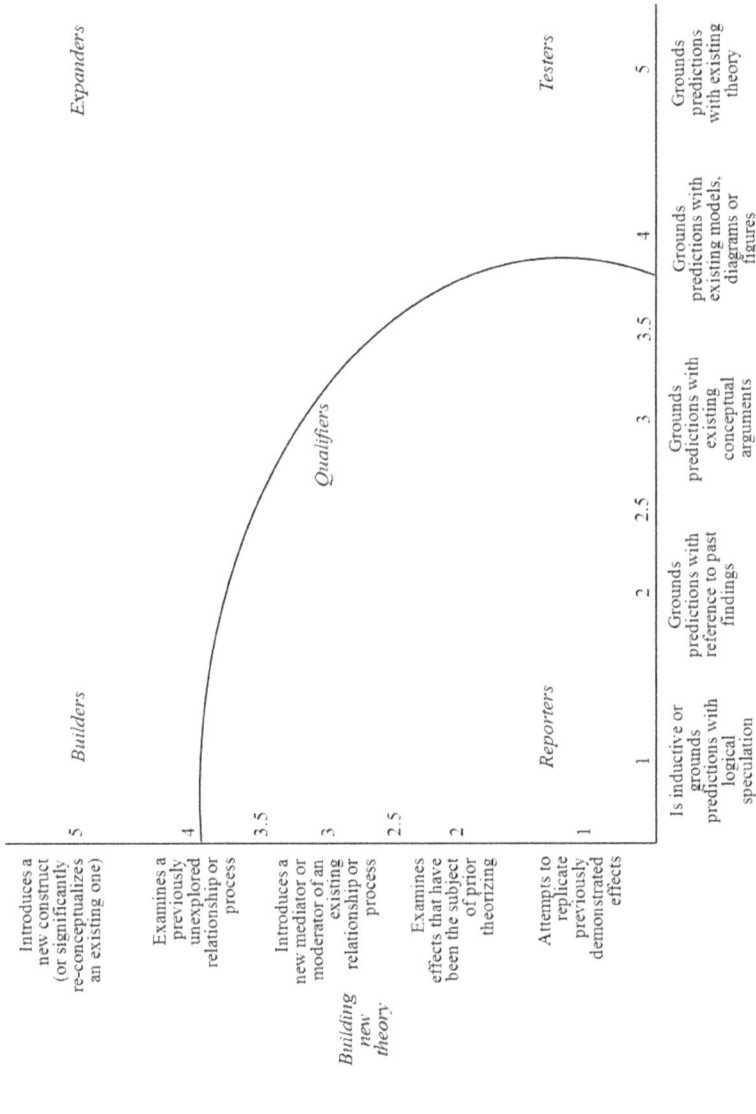

Figure 5.1 A typology of theoretical contributions for empirical articles

Table 5.4 Method categorisation of tourist behaviour-related articles published in four Chinese journals, 2006–2013

	Tourism Tribune	Tourism Science	Human Geography	Economic Geography	Total
Pure description/simple statistical analysis	12	6	4	2	24
Conceptual/basic research	9	2	2	0	13
Complicated statistical analysis (SEM)	30	12	7	3	52
Complicated statistical analysis (non-SEM)	29	26	28	17	100
Qualitative research	2	2	0	0	4
Mixed methods	10	5	0	0	15
Total	92	53	41	22	208

testing) but low levels of theory building (receiving a rating of 1 or 2 on theory building). In contrast with the *tester*, a *builder* is an article that is relatively high in theory building (receiving a rating of 4 or 5 on theory testing) but relatively low in theory testing (receiving a rating of 1 or 2 on theory testing). Finally, in contrast with the *reporter*, an *expander* is an article that is relatively high in both theory building and theory testing (receiving a rating of 4 or 5 on both theory testing and theory building). Such an evaluation indicates that research into tourist market and tourist behaviours in China is still at a developing stage with limited theoretical contributions.

Alternative knowledge contributions

Research can make contributions other than theory development (Lynch *et al.*, 2012; Park, 2012), for instance, seeking straightforward knowledge about the phenomenal world (Brinberg & McGrath, 1985; Lynch *et al.*, 2012; Park, 2012). As there are lots of new tourism industry phenomena in China, better understanding of these phenomena could also justify research contributions (Park, 2012).

Applying Lynch *et al.*'s (2012) criteria to the rest of the 184 empirical tourist market and behaviour articles, we found that the majority of these articles were *describers* and *appliers*. Many tourist behaviour studies attempted to describe, measure and compare tourist perceptions in a wide range of areas, such as destination safety and security, destination attributes, authenticity of cultural products, and accessibility. On the other hand, most of the tourist market studies were dedicated to examining the temporal and spatial structures of different markets. These *describer/applier* articles enable a better understanding of the current market situation and tourist behaviour characteristics; however, there was very little theoretical or methodological advancement in the area. Nevertheless, the contributions of these publications to a better understanding of existing market phenomena should be recognised, especially considering China as a developing country where new tourism industry phenomena keep emerging. As argued by Lynch *et al.* (2012) and Park (2012), phenomenon-driven research should also be valued, as such research helps develop our knowledge on a particular and substantive phenomenon. Such understanding of a new substantive phenomenon may provide a foundation for further theorising around the phenomenon. After all, theory acts as the basic and ultimate goal of scientific research (Kerlinger & Lee, 2000).

It should be noted that methodological/instrumental innovations were witnessed in the tourist market and behaviour studies. For instance, Hu and Bai (2013) developed and validated a measurement scale for tourism destination image restoration; Wang *et al.* (2011) developed the tourist satisfaction index system; and Zhu *et al.* (2011) introduced a geographical concentration index to improve the measurement of tourist density.

Conclusion

Research in tourist markets and tourist behaviours is still in the early development stage (Ballantyne *et al.*, 2009: 150; Sharpley, 2011: 54). Nonetheless, over the eight-year period between 2006 and 2013, tourism academics in China investigated a variety of topics around tourist markets and behaviours. These include market profiles and segmentation, temporal and spatial structures of source markets, market size, market development trends, tourist perceptions/cognition, needs/motivations/expectations, decision-making/destination choice, satisfaction, behavioural intentions, and geographical behaviours. Quantitative methods were widely used in both tourist market and behaviour studies. Mixed methods have also been increasingly used.

The academic contributions of the tourist market and behaviour studies were evaluated. About one-fifth of the empirical tourist market and behaviour articles were identified as theory driven. Among these theory-driven articles, more than 70% were identified as *reporters*, possessing relatively low levels of theory building and theory testing, while the rest were identified as *qualifiers*, showing moderate levels of theory building and theory testing quality. Unfortunately, no article was identified as a *tester* or *builder* or *expander*, representing high levels of theoretical contribution. The rest of the empirical articles were also evaluated in terms of the alternative contributions to understanding a substantive phenomenon. The majority of these articles were identified as *describers* and *appliers*, which undoubtedly have contributed to our understanding of China's tourism development. In addition, some methodological/instrumental contributions in terms of measurement scale development and methodological advancements have been identified. Despite all these developments, there still seems to be a long way to go for tourism academics in China to develop fine-grained tourist behaviour and market knowledge through rigorous, insightful and quality research practice.

References

Bacharach, S.B. (1989) Organizational theories: Some criteria for evaluation. *Academy of Management Review* 14 (4), 496–515.

Bai, K. (2010) A study on the relationship between place attachment and tourists' loyalty in rural tourism destinations. *Human Geography* 25 (4), 120–125.

Bai, K. and Guo, S. (2010) Study on the impact of inbound tourists' emotional experience on their loyalty – a case study of Islamic traditional community in Huifang, Xi'an. *Tourism Tribune* 25 (12), 71–78.

Bai, K. and Ma, Y. (2007) A study on the shopping preference behaviour of tourists: A case of inbound tourists in Xi'an. *Tourism Tribune* 22 (11), 52–57.

Bai, K., Ma, Y. and You, X. (2008) Reflections on the conception of tourist perception and cognition based on researches of tourist behaviours. *Tourism Science* 22 (1), 22–28.

Ballantyne, R., Packer, J. and Axelsen, M. (2009) Trends in tourism research. *Annals of Tourism Research* 36 (1), 149–152.

Bao, G. and Hu, F. (2008) A study on the impact of destination tourism image on tourists' after-sale behaviour: An analysis of perspectives from Japanese and Korean tourists in Hangzhou. *Tourism Tribune* 23 (10), 40–46.

Bao, J., Chen, G. and Ma, L. (2014) Tourism research in China: Insights from insiders. *Annals of Tourism Research* 45, 167–181.

Brinberg, D.L. and McGrath, J. (1985) *Validity and the Research Process*. Beverly Hills, CA: Sage Publications.

Campbell, J.P. (1990) The role of theory in industrial and organizational psychology. In M.D. Dunnette and L.M. Hough (eds) *Handbook of Industrial and Organizational Psychology* (pp. 39–74). Palo Alto, CA: Consulting Psychologists Press.

Chen, C.-C., and Petrick, J.F. (2013) Health and wellness benefits of travel experiences: A literature review. *Journal of Travel Research* 52 (6), 709–719.

Chen, G. and Bao, J. (2011) Progress on overseas studies on China's tourism: A review from the perspective of academic contributions. *Tourism Tribune* 26 (2), 28–35.

Chen, G. and Huang, Y. (2008) Influencing factors on tourists' revisit decision-making: A web-based empirical study. *Tourism Tribune* 23 (11), 69–74.

Chen, G. and Huang, Y. (2010) An empirical study on tourists' motivation to revisit urban destinations: A case study of Xiamen. *Tourism Science* 24 (1), 78–85.

Chen, G., Bao, J. and Huang, S. (2014) Developing a scale to measure backpackers' personal development. *Journal of Travel Research* 53 (4), 522–536.

Chen, Y., Xu, H. and Guo, J. (2013) Satisfaction equilibrium: An analysis of tourist satisfaction and shopping from a supply chain perspective. *Tourism Tribune* 28 (3), 80–86.

Chiu, S., Chen, N. and Zhang, Y. (2011) A study on tourists' perception of crime risk: A case study of international tourists to India. *Tourism Science* 25 (6), 34–45.

Colquitt, J.A. and Zapata-Phelan C.P. (2007) Trends in theory building and theory testing: A five-decade study of the *Academy of Management Journal*. *Academy of Management Journal* 50 (6), 1281–1303.

Corley, K.G. and Gioia, D.A. (2011) Building theory about theory building: What constitutes a theoretical contribution? *Academy of Management Review* 36 (1), 12–32.

Dai, G. and Xiao, L. (2012) Spatial characteristics of event-goers' place identity based on regional relation and IPA model – a case study of the International Horticultural Exposition 2011 in Xi'an. *Human Geography* 27 (4), 115–124.

DiMaggio, P.J. (1995) Comments on 'what theory is not'. *Administrative Science Quarterly* 40, 391–397.

Dong, L. (2011) A study on the origin of heritage tourists' motivation difference. *Tourism Science* 25 (12), 47–57.

Durko, A.M. and Petrick, J.F. (2013) Family and relationship benefits of travel experiences: A literature review. *Journal of Travel Research* 52 (6), 720–730.

Eisenhardt, K.M. (1989) Building theories from case study research. *Academy of Management Review* 14 (4), 532–550.

Fang, Y., Huang, Z., Tu, W. and Wang, K. (2013) Impact of tourism motivation on experience at war memorials: A case study of Nanjing Massacre Memorial Hall. *Tourism Science* 27 (5), 64–75.

Feng, J. (2011) Perceptions of the image of Beijing's tourist destinations – an analysis of the multi-dimensional discourses on the blogs from Chinese and Western tourists. *Tourism Tribune* 26 (9), 19–28.

Feng, S. and Sha, R. (2007) A tentative study on the evaluation model of tourists' perception of the authenticity and satisfaction in ancient village tour. *Human Geography* 22 (6), 85–89.

Gan, L. and Lu, T. (2012) Study on visitors' expectations, use and evaluation to museum interpretation system: An analysis based on knowledge needs. *Tourism Tribune* 27 (9), 56–64.

Gan, L., Liu, Y. and Lu, T. (2010) Study on the motives of tourists coming to Sichuan after Wenchuan earthquake and their perceptions about the impact of the earthquake on local tourism. *Tourism Tribune* 25 (1), 59–64.

Gan, L., Lu, T. and Wang, X. (2013) An empirical study of the domestic tourists' perception on Tibet's tourism image. *Tourism Science* 27 (2), 73–82.

Gao, J., Ma, Y. and Wu, B. (2012) The application of structural equation modelling in tourism research: A review, reflection and examination. *Tourism Tribune* 27 (7), 98–111.

Gao, Y. and Zheng, Y. (2010) A comparative study on the authentic perception of landscapes in Fenghuang Ancient City – from the perspective of residents and tourists. *Tourism Tribune* 25 (12), 44–52.

Gee, C.Y., Choy, D.J.L. and Makens, J.C. (1984) *The Travel Industry*. Westport: AVI.

Guo, W. (2008) A study on the willingness tendency of tourists to participate in the performance of movie and TV tourism: Based on tourists' survey in Tangcheng, Three-kingdom City and Water Margin City, Wuxi. *Tourism Tribune* 23 (10), 61–67.

He, Q. (2011) The inherent mechanism and temporal-spatial feature of China's domestic tourist satisfaction. *Tourism Tribune* 26 (9), 45–52.

He, Q. (2012) A internal mechanism and promotion strategy of tourist satisfaction in coastal cities. *Tourism Science* 26 (5), 65–75.

Hong, Y. and Tao, W. (2006) Tourists' demands for interpretative media: A case study of the museum of the mausoleum of the Nanyue King. *Tourism Tribune* 21 (11), 43–48.

Hu, P. (2008) An empirical research on tourist satisfaction at business tourism destinations: A case study of Xujiahui District in Shanghai. *Tourism Science* 22 (1), 29–33.

Hu, X. and Bai, K. (2013) A study on the tourism destination image restoration scale: A contrast perspective of domestic and inbound tourists integration. *Tourism Tribune* 28 (9), 73–83.

Huang, J. and Han, R. (2010) On the guarantee of tourist rights of Chinese mainland residents travelling to Taiwan – perspective from the comparison of tour model contract across Taiwan Straits. *Tourism Tribune* 25 (8), 65–71.

Huang, X. (2008) Research on expectations of Chinese outbound tourists to Canada: Based on a market survey. *Tourism Science* 22 (2), 44–48.

Huang, X. (2009) A study on temporal-spatial behaviour pattern of tourists based on time-geography science: A case study of the Summer Palace, Beijing. *Tourism Tribune* 24 (6), 82–87.

Huang, X. and Ma, X. (2011) A study on tourists' rhythm of activities based on GPS data. *Tourism Tribune* 26 (12), 26–29.

Huang, Y. and Huang, F. (2007) Tourists' perceived value model and its measurement: An empirical study. *Tourism Tribune* 22 (8), 42–47.

Ji, X. and Chen, J. (2013) Spatial-temporal dynamic changes of inbound tourism market and market expand strategy in Fujian Province. *Economic Geography* 33 (5), 158–164.

Jiang, T. and Hu, J. (2011) On tourist-to-tourist interactions in service contact – based on the technique of critical incident. *Tourism Tribune* 26 (5), 77–83.

Jiang, T. and Zhang, F. (2013) Influence of tourist-to-tourist interaction on re-patronage intention: A tourist experience perspective. *Tourism Tribune* 28 (7), 90–100.

Jiao, Y. (2006) Analysis of the tourist decision model based on the tourist preference and perception risks. *Tourism Tribune* 21 (5), 42–47.

Jin, C., Lu, Y. and Fan, L. (2010) Research on spatial structure of domestic tourism source markets of Jiangsu. *Economic Geography* 30 (12), 2104–2108.

Kerlinger, F.N. and Lee, H.B. (2000) *Foundations of Behavioural Research*. Fort Worth, TX: Harcourt.

Li, C., Wang, Y., Liu, Y., Dong, R. and Zhao, J. (2013) A study of the temporal-spatial behaviour of tourists based on geo-referenced photos. *Tourism Tribune* 28 (10), 30–36.

Li, M. and Xie, H. (2008) A comparative study on the motivational and behavioural characteristics of Chinese and foreign eco-tourists. *Tourism Tribune* 22 (3), 18–23.

Li, S. and Gan, Q. (2011) A study on the perception evaluation system of tourism public service in mega-events – based on the survey from the 16th Asian Games. *Economic Geography* 31 (6), 1047–1053.

Li, W. and Zhang, H. (2010) An empirical study of tourist perceived value model of ancient villages: A case study on Zhangguying Village. *Tourism Science* 24 (2), 55–63.

Li, Y. and Hao, X. (2009) A study on the tourists' spatial travel characters in Xi'an area. *Tourism Tribune* 24 (4), 29–33.

Liang, W. (2009) A study on the tourist communication behaviours between foreign visitors and local residents in Xi'an. *Human Geography* 24 (3), 93–96.

Lin, T. and Hu, J. (2013) Study on the tourists' perception for the authenticity of Shanghai industrial heritage. *Human Geography* 28 (4), 114–119.

Liu, C. and Gao, J. (2007) Analyses on inbound tourism market of Shanghai based on the competition state and the preference scale. *Human Geography* 22 (3), 73–77.

Liu, J., Cheng, S., Chen, Y., Jiang, Y. and Li, J. (2008) Study on tourists' perception of hi-tech tourism resources in park and zone category: A case of Olympic Games Village Hi-tech Park, Chinese Academy of Sciences. *Tourism Tribune* 23 (7), 34–39.

Liu, J., Wang, H. and Chen, R. (2009b) Study on the impact of experiences in ecotourism accommodations and personal involvement on tourists' environmental behavioural intentions. *Tourism Tribune* 24 (8), 82–88.

Liu, L. (2013) Screen-induced tourism: Perceived destination image and intention to visit. *Tourism Tribune* 28 (9), 61–72.

Liu, Y., Zhang, J. and Wang, H. (2007) Analysis on the preference scale and competition state of inbound foreign tourist market of Huangshan city. *Human Geography* 22 (2), 43–47.

Liu, Y., Tang, Y., Tian, G. and Liao, J. (2009a) An empirical study on the evaluation of inbound tourists' satisfaction in Chengdu Research Base of Giant Panda Breeding (CRBGPB). *Tourism Tribune* 24 (3), 36–41.

Lu, J. (2008) The travelling patterns of Taer Lamasery tourists and their impact on local tourism economy. *Tourism Tribune* 23 (12), 29–33.

Lu, S., Pan, H. and Cao, C. (2011) Tourist perceptions on the public transport performance in tourism destination – a case study of Huangshan City. *Human Geography* 26 (6), 133–137, 159.

Luo, F., Zhong, Y., Wu, H. and Zhang, X. (2008) Tourism interpretive demand of visitors in World Natural Heritage Site: Take Wulingyuan as an example. *Tourism Tribune* 23 (8), 69–73.

Luo, Q. and Zhang, A. (2010) Study on food and beverage behaviour of foreign business tourists – taking foreign buyers at Canton Fair as an example. *Tourism Tribune* 25 (7), 47–53.

Luo, S., Huang, Y., Cheng, D. and Ding, P. (2011) Study on the effect of affective factors on tourist experience and satisfaction – taking the performance 'Impression of Liusanjie' in Guilin as an example. *Tourism Tribune* 26 (1), 51–58.

Luo, W., Xu, F., Timothy, D.J., Huang, Y. and Zhang, T. (2013) An analysis of factors influencing the satisfaction of urban visitors: City features, personal characteristics and tourist motives. *Tourism Tribune* 28 (11), 50–58.

Lv, X., Xu, H. and Yang, Y. (2011) Study on tourists' power under the perspective of supply chains. *Tourism Tribune* 26 (11), 34–38.

Lynch, J.G., Jr. (2011) ACR Fellow's address: Substantive consumer research. In D.W. Dahl, G.V. Johar and S.M.J. van Osselaer (eds) *Advances in Consumer Research*, Vol. 38. Duluth, MN: Association for Consumer Research.

Lynch, J.G. Jr., Alba, J.W., Krishna, A., Morwitz, V.G. and Gürhan-Canli, Z. (2012) Knowledge creation in consumer research: Multiple routes, multiple criteria. *Journal of Consumer Psychology* 22, 473–485.

National Science Foundation (1953) What is basic research? See http://www.nsf.gov/pubs/1953/annualreports/ar_1953_sec6.pdf (accessed 31 May 2014).

Pan, L. (2009) An analysis of tourist cognition features of intervening opportunities of tourist destinations. *Human Geography* 24 (6), 103–106.

Park, C.W. (2012) Two types of attractive research: Cute research and beautiful research. *Journal of Consumer Psychology* 22, 299–302.

Pearce, P.L. (2005) *Tourist Behaviour: Themes and Conceptual Schemes*. Clevedon: Channel View Publications.

Peng, D. (2013) A new perspective of tourist experience study: The research on social relationships of tourist-to-tourist interaction. *Tourism Tribune* 28 (10), 89–96.

Qi, Q., Zhang, J., Yang, Y., Lu, S. and Zhang, H. (2009) On environmental attitudes and behaviour intention of tourists in Natural Heritage Site: A case study of Jiuzhaigou. *Tourism Tribune* 24 (11), 41–46.

Qiu, H., Zhou, Q., Zhao, N. and Cheng, L. (2012) A study on differences of sense of place between tourists and locals: A case study of Tunxi old street, Huangshan. *Human Geography* 27 (6), 151–157.

Qiu, M., Wang, F., Sha, R. and Hou, G. (2013) Tourists' perception of and satisfaction with soundscape properties in tourist areas: A case study of Nanjing Confucius Temple-Qinhuai Scenic Area. *Tourism Tribune* 28 (1), 54–61.

Quan, H., Zhao, L., Chen, T. and Yang, Z. (2012) An empirical analysis of tourist structure in the inbound tourism market based on SSM model – a case study on Jiangsu Province. *Economic Geography* 32 (1), 147–152.

Research Group of China Tourist Satisfaction Index (2012) On the construction of tourist satisfaction evaluation system and its empirical study. *Tourism Tribune* 27 (7), 74–80.

Sharpley, R. (2011) *The Study of Tourism: Past Trends and Future Directions*. London and New York: Routledge.

Shen, P. (2012) A study on the effects of social responsibility of tourism enterprises on destination image and tourist loyalty. *Tourism Tribune* 27 (2), 72–79.

Song, Z., Chen, F. and Song, G. (2006) A research on the attraction of world cultural heritage based on tourist perception: A case study of Mountain Tai. *Tourism Science* 20 (6), 28–34.

Su, L. and Huang, F. (2010) A study of service fairness mechanism on tourist loyalty: A case study of sightseeing tourists at Wuyi Mountain. *Tourism Science* 24 (4), 26–39.

Su, L. and Huang, F. (2012) Study on the relationships among destination social responsibility, destination reputation, destination identification and tourism loyalty. *Tourism Tribune* 27 (10), 53–64.

Su, L. and Wang, L. (2007) Market segmentation and positioning research on Chengdu international tourism marketing. *Tourism Tribune* 22 (2), 67–71.

Sui, L., Li, Y. and Cheng, Y. (2010) A study on the value differences of tourists visiting cultural heritages in both China and Western countries: A case study of tourists in Xipan. *Tourism Tribune* 25 (2), 35–41.

Tan, C., Tang, H. and Song, J. (2010) On the relationships between rural tourists' life stress, leisure coping strategies and health. *Tourism Tribune* 25 (2), 66–71.

Tang, X., Huang, X., Xia, Q. and Zheng, J. (2011) The impact of brand personalized characters of traditional ancient villages on tourists' intention of revisit – a case of Shuhe, Zhouzhuang, Langzhong and Pingyao ancient towns. *Tourism Tribune* 26 (9), 53–59.

Tao, W. and Huang, X. (2012) Research on temporal and spatial distribution pattern of inbound tourists and its evolution in Guangdong Province from 2000 to 2009. *Human Geography* 27 (1), 106, 113–118.

Wang, C. and Qu, H. (2013) Empirical study on relationships of travel motivation, destination image and tourist expectation. *Tourism Tribune* 28 (6), 26–37.

Wang, K., Tang, C. and Liu, J. (2011) A measuring model on tourist satisfaction index in cultural creative-type tourism destination: A case of 798 Art Zone in Beijing. *Tourism Tribune* 26 (9), 36–44.

Wang, K., Huang, Z., Fang, Y. and Zhang, H. (2013) Impacts of tourists' involvement on place attachment in cultural tourist attractions. *Human Geography* 28 (3), 135–141.

Wang, L., Zhang, J., Cao, J., Wu, T., Cai, Y. and Yang, Q. (2010) A study on the evaluation of the accessibility of a tourist destination from the perspectives of tourists' perception – a case study of Jiuzhaigou Nature Reserve. *Human Geography* 25 (2), 144–148.

Wang, S., Hu, R. and Li, R. (2010) The use of importance-performance analysis for evaluating China as an international tourist destination – based on American leisure tourists' perception. *Tourism Tribune* 25 (5), 44–50.

Wang, Y. (2006) An investigation on domestic leisure and holiday-making. *Tourism Tribune* 21 (6), 58–65.

Wen, S. and Wei, D. (2012) A study on tourists' willingness to pay for educational services in sightseeing places. *Economic Geography* 32 (10), 170–176.

Whetten, D.A. (1989) What constitutes a theoretical contribution? *Academy of Management Review* 14 (4), 490–495.

Wu, L. and Hou, X. (2006) A study on the motivation of movie- induced tourists – a case study of tourists in Longquan Villa of Tieling. *Human Geography* 21 (2), 24–27.

Wu, T., Zhang, J. and Li, W. (2010) The impact of regional cultural differences on tourists' perception of tourism destination image. *Tourism Tribune* 25 (6), 66–72.

Xiao, X., Zhang, J., Sun, S. and Zhu, J. (2012) Analysis on the factors effecting tourists' sense of place to calligraphic landscape scenic – a case study of thirteen rock inscriptions of Shimen in Hanzhong, Shaanxi. *Human Geography* 27 (6), 130–136.

Xie, L. and Li, J. (2007) A study of the relationships between tour guides' service quality and tourists' trust and behavioural intentions. *Tourism Science* 21 (4), 43–48, 78.

Xie, L., Han, X. and Gu, B. (2007) The impact of service justice, service quality and organizational image on visitors' behaviour intention. *Tourism Tribune* 22 (12), 51–58.

Xie, X., Ma, Y. and Bai, K. (2010) Analysis of inbound tourists' cognition based on gender differences: A case study of the Yangtze River Delta Region. *Tourism Science* 24 (6), 47–54.

Xie, Y. and Yu, Z. (2010) On the methodological issues related to the application of SEM in China's tourism research. *Tourism Tribune* 24 (3), 20–28.

Xin, S., Tribe, J. and Chambers, D. (2013) Family and relationship benefits of travel experiences: A literature review. *Annals of Tourism Research* 41, 66–88.

Xu, F. (2008) Market segmentation and positioning research on Chengdu international tourism marketing. *Tourism Tribune* 23 (2), 36–40.

Xu, J. (2007) An analysis of the needs and behaviour of holiday-makers: Taking Chinese and Russian tourists to Sanya as an example. *Tourism Tribune* 22 (12), 59–65.

Yao, J., Chen, B. and Tian, S. (2008) Study on tourists' perception of rural travel quality in ethnic region: A case study of Dushi Farm, Changji Prefecture, Xinjiang. *Tourism Tribune* 23 (11), 75–81.

Yao, Y. and Luo, Y. (2006) An analysis of the TPB model of tourists' destination choice. *Tourism Tribune* 20 (5), 20–25.

Yu, Y., Tian, J. and Su, J. (2010) A study of the relativity between place attachment and post-tour behavioural tendencies of visitors: Taking value perception and satisfaction experience as intermediary variables. *Tourism Science* 24 (2), 54–62, 74.

Zhang, C. and Bai, K. (2011) Brand personality of rural tourism destinations and tourists' loyalty: Mediating effect of place attachment. *Tourism Tribune* 26 (2), 49–57.

Zhang, C. and Gao, J. (2007) Analyses on inbound tourism market of Shanghai based on the competition state and the preference scale. *Human Geography* 22 (3), 73–77.

Zhang, H., Lu, L. and Zhang, J. (2006) The influence of an analysis of the perceived distance on tourism destination image – A case study of the perceived image of tourist in five origin cities on Zhouzhuang, Suzhou. *Human Geography* 21 (5), 25–30, 83.

Zhang, H., Zhang, J., Cao, J., Liu, C., Shi, C. and Yang, Y. (2008) A study on random coefficient Logit model about tourists' destination choice based on their travel motivation. *Tourism Tribune* 23 (6), 43–47.

Zhang, H., Lu, L., Cai, L. and Huang, Z. (2011a) Tourism destination image structural model and visitors' behavioural intentions: Based on a confirmatory study of localization of potential consumers. *Tourism Science* 25 (1), 35–45.

Zhang, H., Zhang, J., Shi, C. and Liu, Z. (2011b) An analysis of the interaction between tourists' cognitive distance and their satisfaction. *Human Geography* 26 (5), 117–120, 142.

Zhang, L., Wu, C., Peng, Y. and Zhao, H. (2010) Research on interpretation demand at geological relics sights: A case study of Cuihuashan National Geo-park in Shaanxi Province. *Tourism Science* 24 (6), 39–46, 54.

Zhang, T. (2012) A study on the effect of food tourism motivation on tourist satisfaction and behavioural intention. *Tourism Tribune* 27 (10), 78–84.

Zhang, X., Zhang, S. and Ma, X. (2006) A study on the behaviour of self-driving tourists in China. *Tourism Tribune* 21 (9), 31–35.

Zhang, Y. (2008) An empirical study on visitors' behaviour trend after travel: A case of leisure tourists in Qingdao. *Tourism Tribune* 23 (3), 74–78.

Zhang, Y. and Ma, Y. (2007) An analysis of tourists' perception based on image modification: A case study of Japanese market into China. *Tourism Tribune* 22 (10), 12–15.

Zhao, H. and Wu, B. (2013) A study on the relationship between place identity and leisure benefits for individual visitors from Mainland China to Taiwan. *Tourism Tribune* 28 (12), 54–63.

Zhao, M., Shao, L. and Lin, Y. (2013) Perceptional differences of urban space between visitors and local residents: A case study of west towns in Nanhai, Guangdong Province. *Tourism Science* 27 (2), 46–58.

Zhao, X. (2009) An empirical study of dispersed choice in tourism destinations based on tourist specific properties: A case study of transit inbound tourists in three ports. *Tourism Tribune* 24 (12), 60–65.

Zhou, H., Xu, C. and Tang, Q. (2010) Study on the relationship among cognitive gap, emotion and tourist's place attachment. *Human Geography* 25 (5), 132–136.

Zhou, L., Cheng, X. and Zhou, T. (2006) A research on the willingness to pay for certificated ecotourism product: The empirical analysis based on the tourists of Zhejiang's four scenic spots. *Economic Geography* 26 (1), 140–144.

Zhu, Q., Li, Z. and Yang, X. (2011) An improvement of evaluating method on tourist concentration degree with geographic concentration index. *Tourism Tribune* 26 (4), 26–29.

Zou, Y. and Zheng, X. (2012) An empirical study on the affecting factors of tourists' sense of security in tourist destinations – a case study of Quanzhou, Fujian Province. *Tourism Tribune* 27 (1), 49–57.

6 Tourist Attraction Management in China: Issues and Challenges

Introduction

China has a unique and complicated institutional system managing its tourism resources and attractions. A lot of issues have been discussed and debated in a heated way with regard to tourist attraction management in China. In most cases, as tourist attractions based on natural and cultural resources (e.g. mountains, water and cultural heritage) are state-owned and thus remain as state assets, local (provincial and sub-provincial) governments, in the context of political decentralisation, are heavily involved in the management of these attractions. The management of these attractions has also been influenced by China's general reform roadmap on state-owned enterprises, government system restructuring and fiscal reform. Tourism researchers in China have examined various topics pertaining to tourist attractions management in China. Four major areas that have been exposed to heated academic discussions are: (1) governance models; (2) admission ticketing; (3) environment and ecological system management; and (4) safety and risk management. These topics are reviewed and discussed in this chapter. In each topic, the emerging issues and challenges that have been identified and discussed in the literature are elaborated on. In addition, emerging areas for future research are provided.

Governance Models

Governance refers to all processes of governing; it can be undertaken by a government, market or network, over a family, tribe, formal or informal organisation or territory, or through laws, norms, power or language (Mark, 2013). It pertains to processes and decisions that aim to define behaviours, grant power and verify performance. The governance model, as an academic term, has been used interchangeably with the terms *development model* and *governance strategy* in the tourism literature in China (Wang & Xing, 2009). The governance model encompasses interaction strategies through which public and private stakeholders seek to achieve common objectives and make decisions (Gill & Williams, 2011). Tourist attractions in China can generally be classified into three basic categories considering the attraction type, ownership of the resources, main investor, land use and management structure. The first category refers to attractions that are established within or territorially overlapping with national protected areas (cultural, natural or a mix), for instance, National Forest Parks, National Historic and Scenic Areas, National Geological Parks, National Nature Reserves, National Marine Parks, National Mine Parks and National Archaeological Parks, among others. The concept of the National Park has been very popular and is often used to cover different types of national protected areas in the Chinese tourism literature; this seems to be stimulated by the worldwide expansion and implementation of national park systems (especially the management systems in National Parks in the United States, Canada and the UK) and the growing recognition of better management and utilisation of protected areas in China. The second category of attractions refers to tourist resorts. Tourist resorts, often based on natural landscape resources like beaches or hot springs, represent an emerging attraction type. In addition to its core attraction features (e.g. beaches, hot springs), the construction of a tourist resort usually requires a huge amount of capital investment and substantial land use. The third category of attractions are those established within or adjacent to ethnic villages. Due to differences in attraction type, resource ownership, investment, land use and management structures, issues and challenges pertaining to the governance model vary across these three categories of tourist attractions.

Governance models in protected areas

With regard to the governance models in protected areas, research works in China have reflected on the following types: (1) evaluating and debating management and business models in various protected area contexts; and (2) learning from national park management experience in the United States, Canada and the UK in order to develop the Chinese national park system. As a typical example of the first type of research, Lin *et al.* (2006) investigated the impacts of the so-called 'closed-end management model' on stakeholders in Wuyishan, a World Cultural and Natural Heritage Site in Fujian Province. As core arrangements in this model, the local government would reallocate the villagers living in the heritage zone, apply traffic regulations to the heritage site, set up assigned entry and exit points to direct visitor flows, and manage tickets sales. The study showed that the surveyed stakeholder groups held different attitudes towards this management model (Lin *et al.*, 2006). While a majority of the employees in the state-owned management company expressed their support for the model, local residents, drivers and tour guides mostly disagreed with this model. In particular, local residents and tour guides felt resentful towards the reallocation plan and the ticketing schedules. Lin *et al.* (2006) suggested that an ideal model should reflect a collaborative type of management wherein all the stakeholders' interests are recognised. Similarly, in the setting of lake tourism, Xu (2006) proposed a polycentric management model, in which stakeholders including the industry, government, academics, residents and media agencies, work in a collaborative way to fulfil their respective duties. In another study, Shi *et al.* (2007) evaluated the business model of the Jiuzhaigou National Nature Reserve, also a World Natural Heritage Site. They argued that under the arrangement that the management company is jointly owned between the government agency Jiuzhaigou Administrative Bureau and the collectivity of local villagers by a share ratio of 51:49, both local villagers' interests and natural resources in the reserve can be effectively protected. However, the dual role played by the Jiuzhaigou Administrative Bureau as both policy maker and product provider seems to have caused low efficiency in the management of this World Heritage Site (WHS) and somehow impacted on its sustainable development (Shi *et al.*, 2007).

It should be noted that such a governance model featuring the local government's dominant role is very common in China. There are both political and historical reasons for this. First of all, the successive fiscal reforms initiated in the early 1990s in China required that national parks in China be transformed into self-financed public institutions; that is, they should not rely on fiscal allocation to support their operations. Since then, national parks in China have all been involved in tourism development to generate revenues. At the same time, the administrative bureaus of national parks in China were granted the right to make institutional policies for the management of national parks, as China's political decentralisation enabled more local government administrations to take charge of policy-making issues.

Such changes and transitions have presented unprecedented challenges to the authorities in charge of national park administration in China. Governance reform is one of the hot issues that have been widely debated in the Chinese tourism literature. Consequently, many scholars turn to study national park development experiences, especially governance models in national parks in Western countries like the United States (e.g. Li, 2010; Zhang & Wang, 2010), Canada (Huang, 2008) and the UK (Cheng et al., 2013). As is widely recognised, the national park administration systems in the United States and Canada represent a central government dominant management model. One of the core elements of national park management in these countries is the establishment of a centralised and specialised government body, such as the *National Park Service* in the United States and *Parks Canada* in Canada, to manage all national parks across the country. Both the *National Park Service* and *Parks Canada* are independent of local governments in terms of fiscal budgets, park planning and designing and daily management. However, as many scholars have discussed, the situation in China is much more complicated. Many obstacles and challenges exist on the way towards a unified and specialised national park management system; various issues have been discussed in the Chinese literature.

Firstly, the different types of nationally designated parks or protected areas are actually supervised by different central government agencies (Table 6.1). Specifically, the National Forest Parks and National Wetland Parks are designated and supervised by the State Forestry Administration. The National Historic and Scenic Areas are designated and supervised by the Ministry of Housing and Urban-Rural Development; the National Geological Parks and National Mine Parks by the Ministry of Land and Resources; the National Marine Parks by the National Bureau of Oceanography; the National Water Conservancy Scenic Areas by the Ministry of Water Resources; and the National Archaeological Parks and National Cultural Relic Protection Key Units by the State Administration of Cultural Heritage. In the designation and administration of National Nature Reserves, seven different central government agencies are involved; these include the State Forestry Administration, the Ministry of Environmental Protection, the National Bureau of Oceanography, the Ministry of Land and Resources, the Ministry of Agriculture, the Ministry of Water Resources, and the Chinese Academy of Sciences. Interestingly, inside many national parks, there are other parks that are nominated and administered by a different central government agency. For example, Xu and Tian (2010) noted that within the Hexigten National Geological Park in Inner Mongolia, there are two National Nature Reserves, five provincial nature reserves, two National Forest Parks, one National Historic and Scenic Area, and two National

Table 6.1 Profile of the nationally designated parks in China

Types	Supervising agencies	Number	By the year
National Forest Park	State Forestry Administration	779	2013
National Wetland Park	State Forestry Administration	298	2012
National Historic and Scenic Area	Ministry of Housing and Urban-Rural Development	225	2012
National Geological Park	Ministry of Land and Resources	240	2014
National Mine Park	Ministry of Land and Resources	72	2013
National Marine Park	National Bureau of Oceanography	28	2014
National Water Conservancy Scenic Area	Ministry of Water Resources	588	2014
National Archaeological Park	State Administration of Cultural Heritage	24	2013
National Key Units of Cultural Relic Protection	State Administration of Cultural Heritage	4295	2013
National Nature Reserve	Seven different central government agencies[a]	356	2012

Notes: [a]These are the State Forestry Administration (251 sites), the Ministry of Environmental Protection (47 sites), the National Bureau of Oceanography (35 sites), the Ministry of Land and Resources (11 sites), the Ministry of Agriculture (10 sites), the Ministry of Water Resources (two sites), and the Chinese Academy of Sciences. Besides, in China, one nationally designated park might be given many different designative titles; for instance, the Zhangjiajie National Forest Park, established in 1982, was the first of its type and has been successively designated as a National Geological Park, National Historic and Scenic Area, and National Nature Reserve, within its exact territory or overlapping areas. Thus the total number of the nationally designated parks in this table might be larger than the number of actual sites.

Cultural Relic Protection Key Units. The varying political and economic interests among different central government agencies have made it very difficult to establish a unified and specialised central agency to take full responsibility for the management of all national parks in China (Lu, 2014; Zhang & Wang, 2010).

Secondly, apart from designation and nominal macro-supervision, the central government agencies have detached themselves from the micro-management and development of the national parks under their authority (Shi et al., 2007). According to the fiscal reform arrangements along the political decentralisation since the 1990s (Cao, 2011; Walder, 1995; Zhou, 2006), national parks are more closely related to local governments in their locations in specific management affairs and are increasingly seeking self-financing solutions through their own management teams. Tourism development on the national park resources, mostly facilitated by the authoritative *national park* entitlement, has been not only a revenue source for the parks to sustain themselves, but also an additional source of income for local governments. Such a situation also obstructs the pathway for the Chinese central government to establish a unified and centralised national park system (Chen, 2009; Lu, 2014; Luo & Bao, 2013; Zhang & Wang, 2010).

Thirdly, multiple stakeholders' interests have been involved in the designation of national parks in China. As Luo and Bao (2013) noted, the initiation and designation of the National Forest Parks has been driven by a number of considerations. These considerations include: (1) releasing the financial burdens on park management due to fiscal reforms; (2) creating economic benefits for both the local residents and the park management; and (3) to a certain degree, reinforcing the administrative power and reach of the supervising central government agency. Due to these considerations, there is a tendency to create as many of these 'national' titles for the parks as is practical, irrespective of the real value of the protected areas in tourism appeals. If a centralised national park system following a unified set of assessment criteria were in place, most of the current entitled national parks would have been disqualified and excluded from the list. In the current political climate in China, any move towards a centralised national parks system would most likely be boycotted by the affected park management authorities themselves as well as the local governments.

Governance models in resort areas and their evolutions

Resorts are places used for relaxation and/or recreation for visitors on vacation. In China, the *National Resort Grading Standard* (NRGS) was promulgated in 2011. According to the NRGS, a resort is defined as an integrated agglomeration of vacation facilities that can satisfy visitors' needs for recreation, health, sports, education and amusement (Chen & Bao, 2013). Resort development in China, especially after the 12 National Tourism Resorts were established in 1992, has seen varied results. While a small number of resorts have been successful, the majority of them have failed. Such an industry scenario attracted a substantial amount of academic attention and a great number of researchers have tried to understand the reasons. In the literature, the resort governance model was identified as one of the key reasons for such failures. Other reasons include the underdeveloped vacation market, undesirable climate at the resort location, and poor construction planning (e.g. Chen & Bao, 2013; Liu, 2007, 2010; Liu & Bao, 2008). Liu (2010) compared the development results of two coastal resorts governed by two different models, the Yalong Bay National Tourist Resort (YBNTR), one of China's most famous and successful resort destinations, and the Beihai Silver Beach National Tourist Resort (BSBNTR), which was considered unsuccessful. The success of the YBNTR was attributed to an enterprise-led governance model which appears to be more adaptable to the market (Liu & Bao, 2008), while the unsuccessful BSBNTR case witnessed excessive administrative intervention by the local government (Liu, 2010). Resort governance models have been evolving along with China's marketisation and modernisation process. In China's economic and institutional transition, resort governance models are susceptible to further change and evolution (Chen & Bao, 2013).

Liu (2007) contended that there were two pathways along which resort governance models in China have been evolving. One path is the change of the authorised power of the resort committee, represented by the BSBNTR case; while the other is withdrawing from the resort committee model to the traditional administrative model, with the Hangzhou Zhijiang National Tourist Resort as a representative case. However, looking into the successful development case of the YBNTR, one may find neither of the two pathways. The governance structure of the YBNTR has changed from a local government-dominated model (1988–1995) (Liu, 2010; Liu & Bao, 2008) to a model featuring a dominant role played by a main developer and a cooperative role by the local government (1995–2008) (Liu & Bao, 2008), and finally transitioning to a model featuring the return of the local government in the leading position of the resort development supported by the resort developer (Chen & Bao, 2013). Examining the evolution of the resort governance model in the YBNTR, Chen and Bao (2013) identified a path-dependence pattern in its evolution. The authors found that, at the key time junctures for decisions on the YBNTR governance models, influential actors (e.g. local government, the developers, and nearby communities) were provided with multiple options. However, the existence of institutional costs delimited the potential options of the actors. In addition, institutional legacy and interest groups' (the main developer versus villagers) bargaining capacities also influenced institutional costs and returns in different directions. These also conditioned the evolution trajectories of selected governance models.

Governance models and their dilemmas in ethnic villages

The literature on governance models in ethnic villages as tourist attractions seems to slightly overlap with that on community participation in tourism development as reviewed in Chapter 4. However, this section will focus on studies pertaining to governance models as interaction strategies through which public and private stakeholders seek to achieve common objectives and make decisions (Gill & Williams, 2011; Wang & Xing, 2009). In this topic area, academic works can be summarised into the following three aspects: (1) identification of the features of different governance strategies; (2) discussion of the dilemmas in village tourism governance; and (3) attempts to seek better governance approaches.

The core tourist attraction features of an ethnic village include residential architecture, folklore and ethnic lifestyles. However, such attractions are common pool resources, which often cause the 'tragedy of the commons', especially in terms of protecting the cultural and natural landscapes (He, 2010; Wang & Liao, 2013; Wang & Liu, 2009). In economics, a common-pool resource is a type of good consisting of a natural or human-made resource system, whose size or characteristics make it costly, but not impossible, to exclude potential beneficiaries from obtaining benefits from its use (Ostrom, 1990). The 'tragedy of the commons' is an economics theory (Hardin, 1968), which contends that individuals acting independently and rationally according to each one's self-interests behave contrary to the whole group's long-term best interests by depleting some common resource. Therefore, the situations in ethnic villages often constitute a dilemma of collective actions toward a collaborative protection of the cultural and natural landscapes on which village tourism is based (Wang, 2009b; Wang & Liao, 2013). In addition, due to the asymmetric power relations among major stakeholders, conflicts among major stakeholders also pose a significant challenge to ethnic village attraction governance. In China's political system, governments are endowed with the greatest power; comparatively, the villagers are in a weak position to counterbalance the power of the state. Under such circumstances, villagers can rarely participate in the decision-making in tourism development, and local governments tend to overlook villagers' interests, causing conflicts and tensions between villagers and local governments (Wang & Liao, 2013). Similarly, external investors encouraged by the local government to develop village tourism share some common power, interests and goals with the local government, and accordingly may exhibit similar behaviour towards the villagers. It is observed that conflicts and tensions between villagers and external developers have also increased (He, 2010; Wang & Liao, 2013).

Solving these dilemmas and seeking better governance and sustainable tourism development has become a significant research issue. In this respect, a number of scholars have reviewed a variety of cases and proposed their suggestions, mainly based on the theory of community empowerment (Scheyvens, 1999, 2002; Sofield, 2003), the theory of cultural rights (Liu & Wang, 2008; Zhang, 2005), and the theory of self-organisation (Ostrom,

1990; Sun, 2004; Wang & Liao, 2013). Specifically, the following are recommended:

- Institutional empowerment to ensure villagers' participation in tourism development in terms of decision-making and benefit sharing. For instance, Wang (2009b) argued that institutional arrangements that ensure villagers' residual claim rights and residual control rights should be in place in order to encourage villagers to protect common resources voluntarily. Wang and Liu (2009) proposed that an autonomous governance mechanism should be established within a village. Similarly, Wang and Liao (2013) reviewed the empowerment practices in Pingan village in Guangxi, and demonstrated that a self-governing system in village tourism is possible and has actually been established by the local community through setting up tourism administration organisations, practitioner organisations and non-profit organisations.
- Cultural empowerment to strengthen villagers' cultural self-consciousness and address the significance of local knowledge in village tourism governance. The theory of cultural rights emphasises the rights of an ethnic group to innovate, sustain and develop their own culture, participate in cultural activities, and gain economic benefits from development. Following such a theory, Liu and Wang (2008) proposed that a guarantee system of cultural rights should be established to stimulate ethnic groups to spontaneously protect and utilise their cultural resources. Similarly, He (2010) noted that each ethnic minority may have their own knowledge in dealing with human–nature and human–human relationships, which can be critical to sustainable village tourism development and governance. Therefore, local knowledge should be addressed and utilised in village tourism development and governance.

Admission Ticketing

In China, most resource-based tourist attractions, especially those established upon public resources such as national protected areas and heritage sites, are owned by the state and thus remain as state assets. In recent years, ticket prices of resource-based tourist attractions have been soaring. Around the issues of admission ticketing in resource-based tourist attractions, there have been heated public debates among academics and industry practitioners. Tourist attraction ticketing issues, therefore, have emerged as a significant research area of tourist attraction management in China. Topic areas that have been frequently studied include: (1) issues in admission ticketing in tourist attractions; (2) factors that influence attraction ticket prices; (3) ticket pricing models; and (4) ticket charging models.

Issues in admission ticketing and influencing factors

Many articles examining issues in relation to admission ticketing are dedicated to analysing the problems and challenges that exist in admission ticketing in tourist attractions. The problems and challenges could be summarised as follows: (1) overuse of ticketing, which means that too many attraction spots with natural views or cultural landscapes have become gated in order to apply admission tickets to visitors (Gao, 2009; Song, 2008); (2) unreasonably high ticket prices, in other words, the ticket prices for some attractions are much higher than ordinary people can afford (Liu & Gan, 2007; Song, 2008); (3) over-dependency on ticket income, which means that charging tickets is the major and even the only source of income for some attractions; conversely, this negatively impacts tourism development at these attractions (Gao, 2009; Liu & Gan, 2007; Song, 2008).

Several researchers have moved away from examining general admission ticketing issues in tourist attractions and focused instead on exploring the factors that influence the ticket prices for tourist attractions. For instance, Huang (2007) analysed the ticket price data (for the year 2004) of a total of 1814 tourist attractions, identifying seven factors that affect ticket pricing. These factors include the accredited grade of the attraction (from non-accredited to 5A attraction, as accredited by CNTA), governance model, total land area and product type of the attraction, market environment (number of tourist attractions at the same level in the same province), industry environment (the proportion of total tourism income in the provincial GDP), and socio-economic environment (per capita GDP in the province). Furthermore, Li *et al.* (2013: 95) developed an econometric model to examine the impacts of the carrying capacity load (defined as the ratio of visitor number over an attraction's optimal capacity) of public resource-based tourist attractions on their ticket price, using data (between 2002 and 2010) from 59 key tourist attractions monitored by the National Holiday Office. The analysis showed that the average carrying capacity load of urban tourist attractions had an effect on ticket prices; however, the effect was marginal and negative; that is to say, ticket price decreases as carrying capacity load rises. This effect does not seem to apply to WHS. According to Li *et al.* (2013), a number of WHS attractions claim that they have applied high ticket prices in order to regulate and control tourist flows for heritage protection; such a claim, however, has been interpreted by the researchers to be an excuse for these WHS attractions to take advantage of their WHS entitlements to manipulate ticket prices (Li *et al.*, 2013).

Ticket pricing models and ticket charging models

Recognising the complexity of ticketing in public resource-based attractions, researchers have recently examined the models for ticket pricing and ticket charging approaches. With regard to ticket pricing models, Guo and Dong (2010) present a mathematical model which takes into account two types of tourism resource ownership (state-owned and privately-owned) and multiple stages (seasons) of tourism development; Lei *et al.*'s (2012) multi-target model considers multiple development goals such as goals for profit, ecological carrying capacity and social welfare; Wei and Deng's (2007) gaming model attempts to determine the optimal ticket price for resource-based attractions applying game theory; Liu *et al.* (2012) elaborate on a systematic dynamics model which discloses the main factors of ticketing and the relationships between them and ticketing prices. These factors include general individual income, number of tourist attractions in the market, price regulation imposed by the government, and the life-cycle of the tourist attraction, among others.

With regard to ticket charging approaches, Yimiti *et al.* (2009) evaluate the efficiency of the 'one ticket system' (unified ticketing approach). There are two forms of ticketing in this system: the 'pure one ticket system' (pure bundling) and the 'mixed one ticket system' (mixed bundling). The former requires tourists to purchase the package ticket for the entire attraction, while the latter gives visitor options to choose from different packages (combinations) of a number of attractions in a large destination/attraction region. It is demonstrated by the authors that the efficiency of the unified ticketing approach depends upon the validity period of the package ticket, the reservation price and reservation time. Reservation time refers to the time that a tourist should spend in the attraction for a pleasant visit, while likewise, reservation price refers to the money that a tourist is willing to pay for such a reservation time. Furthermore, the authors prove that the 'mixed one ticket system' seems to be more efficient than the 'pure one ticket system' in terms of profit returns to the tourist attraction (Yimiti *et al.*, 2009).

Using a qualitative study approach, Wu *et al.* (2013) identify four admission-charging models in historical towns and compare their application contexts and conditions. The models are: (1) the 'fully enclosed' model with a 'one ticket system' for the entire gated attraction; (2) the 'half-closed' model with a nominal one ticket system whereby tourists who consume a certain amount in the attraction are exempted from the ticket charge; (3) the 'half-opened' model that does not require a unified ticket for the entire attraction but a separate ticket for each gated area in the attraction; and (4) the 'fully opened' model with free admission.

Environment and Ecological System Management

Tourism development exerts a significant impact on the environment and ecological systems in and around tourist attractions, especially nature-based attractions. How to apply effective environmental and ecological system management to minimise or mitigate the negative environmental impacts of tourism development is important to the sustainable development of tourist attractions. Managing the environment and ecological systems within tourist attractions still remains an under-researched area in the broader literature of tourist attraction management in China. A small number of articles, however, have serendipitously tapped into the following topics:

- ecological safety assessment and solutions;
- water management;
- assessment of low-carbon attractions;
- environmental behaviour of tourism enterprises; and
- environmental carrying capacity.

Considering the interdisciplinary nature of this area of enquiry, Chinese researchers may have published relevant research in journals specialising in environment and ecological studies. Therefore, the small number of publications in these topics in tourism journals should be interpreted cautiously.

Specifically, the ecological safety issues were examined by some researchers (e.g. Long *et al.*, 2006; Wang *et al.*, 2009). Generally, the issues examined in this aspect include:

- ecological safety management in the general park management system;
- construction of ecological protection infrastructure;
- environmental education;
- environment and ecological monitoring systems; and
- legislative and policy development.

Furthermore, Wang *et al.* (2007) investigated the driving forces behind the water environment management systems in three representative mountain attractions, namely the Yellow Mountain (Anhui Province), Kuniujiang

(Anhui Province) and Putuoshan (Zhejiang Province). They developed an effective water environment management model integrating the following three aspects: stakeholders' consciousness of water environment management, policy-making and its implementation, and technology improvement and management. The concept of low-carbon tourist attractions has become popular in China in recent years; two relevant studies were identified, with one constructing a conceptual model and an evaluative system of low-carbon tourist attractions (Li & Yin, 2012), and another evaluating the low-carbon service efficiency in Zhangjiajie City (Liu, 2012). Wang *et al.* (2012) measured the organisational environmental behaviours of hotels in Wulingyuan National Historic and Scenic Area using a self-constructed scale. The study demonstrated that the motivation for pursuing profits, pressures from the government's environmental regulations and other stakeholders are the main driving factors behind hotels' environmental behaviour. As a sustainable tourism management indicator, environmental carrying capacity has also been a recent research topic. For instance, Yin *et al.* (2013) applied a refined approach (i.e. the dynamic improved analytic hierarchy process) to measure the environmental carrying capacity of the Chongqing Huangshui National Forest Park.

Safety and Risk Management

Previous studies have demonstrated that tourist safety and security is a key factor in the pre-trip decision-making process and significantly affects post-trip satisfaction and intention (e.g. Brunt *et al.*, 2000; Zou & Zheng, 2012). From an attraction management perspective, guaranteeing tourists' safety and security is a legal obligation for attraction management (Yang, 2008). Therefore, safety and risk management in tourist attractions has gained growing attention from the public and government in China.

Despite its importance, there has been limited research on safety and risk management in tourist attractions in the Chinese literature. Some researchers such as Yang (2008) argue that tourist attractions should take up the legal obligations prescribed by the Chinese civil law in order to guarantee their tourists' safety and security. Safety and security issues have become more prominent as a common concern shared by both the government and the public since China hosted international mega-events, like the 2008 Beijing Olympics, the 2010 Shanghai World Expo and the 2010 Guangzhou Asian Games. In such a context, Hu (2009) studies safety management in events and event-hosting areas and has identified hidden safety hazards pertaining to the 2010 Shanghai World Expo with his suggestions for safety management. Similarly, Zheng (2007) investigates safety issues with island tourist attractions and recommends some management strategies. As outdoor activities are becoming increasingly popular in association with domestic tourism in China (Zou *et al.*, 2009), risk management and control in such activities emerges as a significant research area. For instance, Xie (2011a, 2011b) explores the causes and types of safety risks in outdoor training programmes, and proposes a safety and security management system for high-risk tourism projects.

Emerging Research Areas

In this section, we discuss two areas for future tourist attraction management research in China, i.e. digital management (smart attraction management), and tourist flow management. In 2004, the Ministry of Housing and Urban-Rural Development in China recommended that the digital attraction development programmes in Huangshan and Jiuzhaigou be included in the Ministry of Science and Technology's key projects. Since then, digital attraction management has been a popular topic among industry practitioners and tourism academics. Some researchers have started to explore digital attraction management as a topic. For instance, Huang (2007) evaluated the functions of the digital management system in Jiuzhaigou National Nature Reserve around nature/environment preservation and tourism. Feng *et al.* (2010) conducted a more comprehensive evaluation on the performances of the 'Digital Jiuzhaigou' programme between 2002 and 2005; issues like natural resources and environment protection, technological advancement, social benefits and financial performance have been examined.

Effectively managing visitor flows appears to be a pressing research need in the general field of attraction management. This can be illustrated in an incident in Jiuzhaigou. On 2 October 2013, the second day of the National Day Holiday Golden Week, more than 4000 visitors were stranded in the Jiuzhaigou National Nature Reserve. As too many visitors entered the park (Jiuzhaigou), and the park management did not have any emergency action plan in place or additional human resources and facility capacities, tourist congestion caused a serious traffic blockage and violent incidents damaging tourism resources and facilities (XinhuaNet, 2013). Some similar cases have been reported at other popular tourist attractions in China. These cases have made urgent the need to seek more effective visitor flow management measures at tourist attractions. Although some studies focus on visitor demand forecasting in specific attractions (e.g. Liao *et al.*, 2013; Liu & Liu, 2011; Liu *et al.*, 2012; Yu *et al.*, 2012), more specific research on visitor flow management needs to be done. Considering tourist attractions in China are diversified in geographical location, landscape characteristics and, more importantly, in terms of the spatial structure and internal transportation structure, more site- or case-specific empirical studies are needed to better understand the temporal-spatial tourist movements within an attraction. Management solutions need to be worked out to deal with the issue.

Conclusion

This chapter aims to provide a critical review of the progress of research in tourist attraction management in China. It reveals that major research areas include governance models, admission ticketing, environment and ecological systems management, and safety and risk management. Obviously, the management of tourist attractions has been influenced by China's general economic reform and transformation of national governance, including the reform roadmap on state-owned enterprises, fiscal reform and government system reorganisation. In addition to these four topic areas, digital attraction management and tourist flow management have been identified as important emerging topics in tourist attraction management in China.

It should be noted that 'management' is a broadly applied social science term and thus 'tourist attraction management' in the Chinese publications covers a wide range of relevant topics. Topic areas such as stakeholder relationship management, marketing management, image management, interpretation and tour guiding management are also related to tourist attraction management. Some of these areas are covered in other chapters of this book, although not inclusively.

References

Brunt, P., Mawby, R. and Hambly, Z. (2000) Tourist victimisation and the fear of crime on holiday. *Tourism Management* 21 (4), 417–424.

Cao, Z. (2011) The vertically decentralized authoritarianism and the mechanisms of political stability in China. *Sociological Studies* 1, 1–40.

Chen, G. and Bao, J. (2013) Path dependence in the development model changes of tourist resorts: A case study of Yalong Bay National Tourist Resort in Sanya, China. *Tourism Tribune* 28 (8), 58–68.

Chen, W. (2009) An exploration of the reform of administrative system of big ruins: Based on the experiences and lessons gained in the reform of administrative system of scenic areas. *Tourism Tribune* 24 (9), 79–84.

Cheng, S., Zhang, J., Hu, J. and Xu, F. (2013) Comparative evaluation of tourism sustainability between national parks in the UK and China: A case study of Jiuzhaigou National Park and New Forest National Park. *Human Geography* 28 (2), 20–26.

Feng, G., Ren, P., Zhu, Z., Ye, B., Li, J. and Jian, D. (2010) Study on comprehensive performance appraisal for 'Digital Jiuzhaigou' based on the management entropy. *Tourism Tribune* 25 (2), 72–78.

Gao, S. (2009) On the reduction of expenses at scenic areas and simplification of price-fixing method. *Tourism Tribune* 24 (6), 60–66.

Gill, A.M. and Williams, P.W. (2011) Rethinking resort growth: Understanding evolving governance strategies in Whistler, British Columbia. *Journal of Sustainable Tourism* 19 (4–5), 629–648.

Guo, Q. and Dong, J. (2010) Study on the fixing of admission pricing model for the protection of resources in scenic spots. *Tourism Tribune* 25 (8), 72–77.

Hardin, G. (1968) The tragedy of the commons. *Science (AAAS)* 162, 1243–1248.

He, J. (2010) Thoughts about tourism development of ethnic minority villages in the outlying poverty-stricken areas: An inspection with Xijiang Qianhu Miao Village, Guizhou as the center. *Tourism Tribune* 25 (2), 59–65.

Hu, P. (2009) Mega-event highlights the importance of safety management: A discussion on the safety management of 2010 Shanghai World Expo. *Tourism Tribune* 24 (1), 9–11.

Huang, P. (2007) Protection and development: An empirical study on the cooperative effect of digital management in heritage sites – taking 'Digital Jiuzhaiguo' as an example. *Tourism Tribune* 22 (8), 23–28.

Huang, X.-T. (2007) A demonstrative study on the influencing factors of fixing admission fees in domestic tourist attractions. *Tourism Tribune* 22 (5), 73–79.

Huang, X. (2008) Study on PAC model in the central vertical-administrative national park based on theory of governance. *Tourism Tribune* 23 (7), 72–80.

Lei, Q., Shao, P. and Lei, L. (2012) Multi-target ticket pricing analysis of tourist attractions in China. *Tourism Tribune* 27 (7), 49–56.

Li, F., He, J. and Li, L. (2013) The impact of the loading intensity of public resource scenery spots on their entrance fees: Evidence from the key scenery spots monitored by the National Holiday Office. *Tourism Tribune* 28 (4), 94–103.

Li, N. (2013) A computer simulation model for visitors' recreational behaviours at tourism attractions: A case study of the Summer Palace. *Tourism Science* 27 (5), 42–51.

Li, X. (2010) Three conceptual frameworks in the process of recreation land management in American National Parks. *Human Geography* 25 (1), 118–122.

Li, X. and Yin, Y. (2012) A conceptual model of low carbon scenic spots and construction of evaluation index system. *Tourism Tribune* 27 (3), 84–89.

Liao, Z., Ge, P., Ren, P., Luo, Y., Zhang, X. and Feng, G. (2013) Research on prediction of tourists' quantity in Jiuzhaigou valley based on AB@G integration model. *Tourism Tribune* 28 (4), 88–93.

Lin, B., Zhang, X., Zhao, S. and Pan, X. (2006) On the problem of the stakeholders adopting close management in Mount Wuyi. *Tourism Tribune* 21 (7), 33–37.

Liu, C. (2012) On the evaluation approach of 'low-carbon tourism' service providing efficiency and its empirical study: Based on the empirical inspection of environmental protection and transport tourism service in Zhangjiajie. *Tourism Tribune* 27 (3), 90–98.

Liu, H. and Liu, J. (2010) On predicting tourists of Shaoshan red tourism scenic spots on gray model. *Economic Geography* 30 (6), 1047–1051.

Liu, J. (2007) Governance structure and changes of Chinese tourism resorts. *Tourism Science* 21 (4), 57–62.

Liu, J. (2010) A comparative study on coastal resort development model: A case study of Yalong Bay in Sanya and Beihai Silver Beach. *Human Geography* 25 (4), 115–119.

Liu, J. and Bao, J. (2008) Study on the development and management model of Yalong Bay holiday-making resort, Sanya and its enlightenment. *Tourism Tribune* 23 (1), 13–18.

Liu, M. and Gan, X. (2007) Research on regulation tactics of the up-pricing of admission tickets scenic spots in China. *Economic Geography* 27 (4), 701–704.

Liu, W. and Wang, R. (2008) A study on the application of cultural rights theory in tourism development in minority community: A case study of Tao Ping Qiang Village in Lixian County. *Tourism Science* 22 (2), 63–68.

Liu, Q., Lei, L. and Shao, P. (2012) Research on ticket pricing of tourist attractions based on system dynamics. *Tourism Science* 26 (4), 39–51.

Liu, S. and Liu, M. (2011) On the essence of the free-admission model of West Lake scenic spots in Hangzhou and an analysis of duplication. *Tourism Tribune* 26 (10), 50–17.

Liu, Z., Qing, F., Ge, P., Ren, P. and Ran, J. (2012) A study on forecasting daily tourist volume at Jiuzhaigou National Park. *Tourism Science* 26 (2), 59–66.

Long, Y., Xiong, X., Huang, H., Huang, M. and Gan, D. (2006) Reasonable design and ecological safety analysis of Wulingyuan core scenic spot in Zhangjiajie. *Economic Geography* 26 (2), 318–321.

Lu, Y. (2014) Innovating national park models: A case study of the East Zhejiang National Park. *Journal of Zhejiang Party School of CPC* 3, 63–70.

Luo, F. and Bao, J. (2013) Evolutional process and characteristics of National Forest Parks in China: A perspective of the logic of state, market and society. *Economic Geography* 33 (3), 165–169.

Mark, B. (2013) *Governance: A Very Short Introduction.* Oxford: Oxford University Press.

Ostrom, E. (1990) *Governing the Commons: The Evolution of Institutions for Collective Action.* Cambridge: Cambridge University Press.

Scheyvens, R. (1999) Ecotourism and the empowerment of local community. *Tourism Management* 20 (2), 245–249.

Scheyvens, R. (2002) *Tourism for Development: Empowering Communities.* Harlow: Pearson Education.

Shi, X., Li, W., Wang, Y. and Zhu, Z. (2007) Natural resource operation mode that can secure the benefit of residents in protected areas: A case study of joint-stock mechanism in Jiuzhaigou Nature Reserve. *Tourism Tribune* 22 (3), 12–17.

Sofield, T.H.B. (2003) *Empowerment for Sustainable Tourism Development.* Oxford: Pergamon.

Song, D. (2008) Breaking the bottleneck of over-dependence on ticket economy in China's tourism market development. *Tourism Tribune* 23 (5), 11–12.

Sun, Z. (2004) *Social Evolution Theory: A Self-organization Perspective.* Beijing: China Social Sciences Press.

Walder, A.G. (1995) Local governments as industrial firms: An organizational analysis of China's transitional economy. *American Journal of Sociology* 101 (2), 263–301.

Wang, C., Wu, C. and Cheng, F. (2009) Probe on ecological security management model of Zhangjiajie National Forest Park. *Economic Geography* 29 (9), 1580–1584.

Wang, K., Li, M. and Ge, Q. (2012) Environmental behaviour of tourism enterprises in the world heritage sites and its driving mechanism: An empirical study on tourist hotels in Zhangjiajie. *Tourism Tribune* 27 (7), 64–73.

Wang, L. (2009a) On the elite governance of cultural heritage in rural tourism communities: Discussion about the election in Pingan Stockaded village, Guangxi Provinces. *Tourism Tribune* 24 (5), 67–71.

Wang, L. and Liao, G. (2013) From dilemma to rationality: A research on self-organization in village heritage tourism – a Case Study of Pingan Village in Northern Guangxi. *Tourism Science* 27 (2), 36–45.

Wang, Q., Yang, X., Huang, Z. and Zhang, J. (2007) A comparison of water environmental management in mountain-type tourist destinations and model construction. *Tourism Tribune* 22 (11), 47–51.

Wang, R. (2009b) On the application of property rights of Barzel in the resources development of ethnic villages: A case study of Taoping Qiang Village, Li County, Sichuan Province. *Tourism Tribune* 24 (5), 31–35.

Wang, R., and Liu, W. (2009) Internal predicament and solution of ethnic village tourism in minority areas: An in-depth inspection based on the particularity view of resources system. *Tourism Science* 23 (3), 1–5.

Wang, R. and Xing, L. (2009) The changes of development models of minority village tourism in the perspective of neo-institutional economics: A case study of Taoping Qiang Village. *Journal of Yunnan Normal University (Humanities and Social Sciences)* 41 (3), 128–133.

Wei, X. and Deng, Z. (2007) Optimal ticket pricing model of the resourceful scenic spots: Based on game theory under leisure constraints. *Tourism Tribune* 22 (4), 62–66.

Wu, W., Zhang, L. and Qiu, F. (2013) Factors influencing tourism ticket charges in ancient villages and towns: Empirical research in Jiangsu, Zhejiang, Shanghai and Anhui. *Tourism Tribune* 28 (8), 34–41.

Xie, C. (2011a) Research on the safety and security management system of high-risk tourism project in our country. *Human Geography* 26 (2), 133–138.

Xie, C. (2011b) Study on the safety risks of outward bound sports based on aggregation and optimal scaling analysis. *Tourism Tribune* 26 (5), 47–52.

XinhuaNet (2013) The Jiuzhaigou Administrative Bureau apologize to the public about the incidents of stranding tourists. See http://news.sohu.com/20131003/n387598409. shtml (accessed 31 May 2014).

Xu, F. (2006) Polycentric management pattern for sustainable tourism development: A study of lake tourism. *Tourism Tribune* 21 (10), 39–44.

Xu, T. and Tian, M. (2010) On the study progress of tourism system of China's National Geologic Parks and several problems required to be urgently studied. *Tourism Tribune* 25 (11), 84–92.

Yang, X. (2008) On the safeguard obligation of scenic area operators to tourists. *Tourism Tribune* 23 (10), 82–86.

Yimiti, H., Mohetaer P. and Tian, X. (2009) The unified ticket policy and its efficiency in scenic areas: An economic analysis based on bundle pricing model. *Tourism Science* 23 (6), 28–34.

Yin, X., Li, J. and Lei, Y. (2013) Assessment of the forest park's tourism environmental carrying capacity: A case study of Chongqing Huangshui National Forest Park. *Human Geography* 28 (2), 154–159.

Yu, X., Zhu, G., Sha, R., Hu, S. and Wang, Li. (2012) Research on forecasting optimization of tourist arrivals in scenic areas based on monthly data: A case study of Huangshan scenic areas. *Economic Geography* 32 (7), 152–158.

Zhang, H. and Wang, Y. (2010) National park model and implications for the development of sustainable nature-based tourism: Yosemite National Park and Koli National Park case studies. *Economic Geography* 30 (1), 156–161.

Zhang, J. (2005) The legal protection of cultural rights: Protecting the cultural rights in tourism development in ethnic minority areas. *Thinking* 4, 29–33.

Zheng, X. (2007) The development and safety management of the coastal island tourism in mainland China. *Human Geography* 22 (4), 86–89.

Zhou, F. (2006) A decade of tax-sharing: The system and its evolution. *Social Sciences in China* 6, 100–115.

Zou, T., Chen, Y. and Hu, X. (2009) Study progress on the safety management of adventure tourism. *Tourism Tribune* 24 (1), 86–92.

Zou, Y. and Zheng, X. (2012) An empirical study on the affecting factors of tourists' sense of security in tourist destinations – a case study of Quanzhou, Fujian Province. *Tourism Tribune* 27 (1), 49–57.

7 Tour Guiding and Interpretation in China

Introduction

Tour guides are important frontline employees in the tourism industry who play multiple roles in providing services to tourists and contributing to the tourist experience (Cohen, 1985; Huang *et al.*, 2010, 2015). In China, tour guiding is a profession that has been heavily regulated and monitored by the government (Huang & Weiler, 2010). Despite the differences in the tour guiding administration systems between China and other countries, little has been known about research into tour guiding and interpretation among scholars in China except for some English publications that talk about tour guiding quality assurance in China (Huang & Weiler, 2010), and tour guiding performance in China (Huang, 2010a; Huang *et al.*, 2010). Notably, these English publications were based on studies conducted by Chinese-origin researchers outside China.

Depending on the legislative and cultural context, a tour guide can be referred to by many alternative nomenclatures, including 'tourist guide', 'tour leader', 'tour escort' and 'tour coordinator' (Black, 2002; Huang, 2015). The World Federation of Tourist Guide Associations (WFTGA) defines a tour guide as a person who guides visitors in the language of their choice and interprets the cultural and natural heritage of an area, and who normally possesses an area-specific qualification usually issued and/or recognised by the appropriate authority (WFTGA, 2003). In China, a tour guide is officially defined as 'a person who holds a tour guide qualification certificate and is entrusted by a tour operator/travel agency to undertake the work of accompanying tour groups (tourists) in visitation activities following a tour arrangement plan' (Quality of Tour Guide Service, 1995: Clause 2.5).

Despite the importance of tour guiding as a seemingly indispensable profession in the tourism industry, especially with mass package group tours, research on tour guides, tour guiding and interpretation cannot claim a mainstream status in tourism studies (Huang & Weiler, 2010). Nevertheless, a substantial body of literature has been developed around tour guiding and interpretation. The recent book, *Tour Guiding Research: Insights, Issues and Implications* (Weiler & Black, 2015), published by Channel View, provides a timely review of this body of literature in the international English-speaking research community. According to Weiler and Black (2015), journal articles dedicated to tour guiding research have experienced a sharp increase since the turn of the century. Specifically, tour guiding research in relation to China and the Greater China Region (including mainland China, Hong Kong, Macao and Taiwan) mainly centres on examinations of tour guide performance and the influence of tour guiding on visitor satisfaction (Weiler & Black, 2015). As noted above, these studies are mainly conducted by researchers outside mainland China. Therefore, there is an apparent gap in that a lot of tour guiding research done by researchers in China still remains unknown to tourism researchers outside China.

This chapter aims to critically review the research on tour guiding and interpretation in China in parallel with what has been done in the international research community in this line of academic enquiry. To set out, we provide a brief overview on the current state of tour guiding and interpretation research internationally in the next section. Then we offer a detailed critical review of the work done by Chinese scholars in tour guiding and interpretation before concluding this chapter.

International Tour Guiding and Interpretation Research

Weiler and Black (2015) provided a comprehensive review of the tour guiding research in the international research community. In the time span of the past 50 years, they identified a total of 280 papers that focus on tour guides or tour guiding. Notably, 91% of these papers were published after 1990. In the literature search, only one edited book (Black & Weiler, 2003) was uncovered as being devoted to tour guiding scholarship. There seems to be a focused interest in studying tour guiding and related issues among a small and dedicated group of researchers in Europe, clearly demonstrated by the biennial conference, The International Research Forum on Guided Tours, and two special issues on guided tours in the

Scandinavian Journal of Hospitality and Tourism (Vol. 12, No. 1 in 2012 and Vol.13, No. 2 in 2013).

Weiler and Black (2015) identified 146 papers on tour guides and guiding research published in scholarly journals. Three leading tourism journals, *Annals of Tourism Research*, the *Journal of Sustainable Tourism* and *Tourism Management*, together published 43 articles out of the 146 papers. In the English academic literature on tour guiding, a few key areas are covered. According to Weiler and Black's categorisation, these themes include: (1) the role of the tour guide; (2) intercultural communication and interpretation; (3) the contribution of tour guiding to sustainability; (4) tour guiding and visitor satisfaction; (5) tour guide training and education; and (6) quality assurance and the accreditation of tour guiding. Similarly, Huang *et al.* (2010) noted that studies on tour guides have mainly focused on tour guides' roles (e.g. Cohen, 1985; Weiler & Yu, 2007; Yu *et al.*, 2002), tour guide performance (e.g. Geva & Goldman, 1991; Mossberg, 1995), tourist satisfaction with tour guide services (e.g. Wong, 2001), and tour guide administration systems (e.g. Dong *et al.*, 2002).

Tour guides take on a variety of roles in performing their jobs. The role or roles required for a tour guide may vary across the tour guiding service contexts. For example, a guide in a museum would be expected to take more of a role as an interpreter or educator than a guide who leads a package tour group to visit a foreign country destination. Cohen (1985) claimed that the two lines of origin of the modern tour guide were the *pathfinder* and the *mentor*. Other roles identified in the literature include interpreter/educator, information giver, leader, motivator/role model, social catalyst, cultural broker/mediator and navigator/protector, among others (Black & Weiler, 2005). There are both social and political influences on the roles of tour guides in a certain cultural sphere. For instance, the Israeli teacher-guide on guided walks aiming to promote the knowledge of the Israelis' native country performs a role as 'an agent of education and culture rather than of leisure and entertainment' according to the 'Israeli condition' (Katz, 1985: 49); similarly, in the Israeli Experience youth study tours, the guide was expected to be a 'role model' more than anything else (Cohen *et al.*, 2002). In addition, the cultural mediation or cultural broker role of tour guides between tourists and hosts is increasingly acknowledged. In this regard, Weiler and Black (2015) proposed a four-domain framework to summarise research on the mediatory role of tour guides to date as follows:

- mediating/brokering physical access;
- mediating/brokering encounters/interactions;
- mediating/brokering understanding; and
- mediating/brokering empathy/emotional access.

Tour guiding also appears to be a highly politicised type of work and susceptible to political ideology in a particular country. As noted by Dahles (2002), tour guides under the Suharto regime in Indonesia followed the politically and ideologically 'correct' narratives and demeanour in their guiding and interpretation, making guiding less of an opportunity to present the 'true' story.

In association with the mediation role of the tour guide is interpretation or interpretive guiding (Huang et al., 2015; Weiler & Black, 2015). Drawing upon knowledge from the fields of communication and museum and heritage studies, tour guide interpretation seems to have grown into a significant body of literature, although one not commonly received by many tourism researchers. It is commonly accepted that interpretation is distinct from education and is intended to reveal meanings and relationships rather than simply communicate factual information (Ham, 1992; Tilden, 1977). A number of interpretation principles were identified in the literature and these principles are believed to be applicable to guided tours to enhance visitor experiences. The following are representative of these interpretation principles:

- Interpretation should be enjoyable.
- Interpretation should engage two or more senses.
- Interpretation should facilitate individual and group involvement, interaction and participation.
- Interpretation should communicate and create relevance to the audience.
- Interpretation should be theme-based and act on themes.
- Interpretation should convey accurate fact-based information that facilitates understanding and provokes thinking and meaning-making.
- Interpretation should make people feel empathy or create emotional resonance.

Apparently, these principles have been developed and tested in mainly Western contexts. In a meta-analysis of 70 peer-reviewed articles published between 1996 and 2009, Skibins et al. (2012) found that most of the interpretation-related studies were undertaken in the USA (60%) or Australia (30%), and 95% of these studies were conducted in Western contexts. Therefore, the above-identified interpretation principles were at best delimited by Western methodologies and knowledge of communications. Whether these principles are equally applicable to Eastern tour guiding practices is yet to be further tested. At least some evidence shows that some principles may not be appreciated by audiences in Eastern contexts.

For instance, Xu *et al.* (2013) questioned the applicability of the Western 'scientific' approach of interpretation that appreciates accuracy in scientific facts in the Chinese context and argued that a more humanistic 'aesthetic' approach of interpretation, using stories, art and poetry to emotionally engage visitors with cultural and natural landscapes, is more appropriate in the Chinese context.

The English literature has also seen a good number of studies, mostly in Western contexts, that relate tour guiding to sustainability. Weiler and Black (2015) summarised the outcomes of tour guiding in contributing to sustainability in three dimensions: (1) enhancing visitors' understanding and appreciation of sites, communities, cultures and environments; (2) influencing and monitoring visitors' behaviours; and (3) fostering visitors' post-visit, pro-environmental and pro-heritage conservation attitudes and behaviours. In this regard, there seems to be little concern in China to relate tour guiding to sustainable development (Hu & Wall, 2012; Huang & Weiler, 2010). Nevertheless, it would be interesting to fill the gap by reviewing the Chinese literature in relation to tour guiding.

The influences of tour guide performance on tourist behaviour such as satisfaction and behavioural intentions have been identified as another sub-theme in tour guiding studies in the English literature (Geva & Goldman, 1991; Huang, 2010a; Huang *et al.*, 2010, 2015; Mossberg, 1995; Weiler & Black, 2015; Wong, 2001; Zhang & Chow, 2004). As noted by Weiler and Black (2015), many recent studies in this stream were conducted in China or in the Greater China context. For instance, Wong's (2001) study examined international tourists' perceived satisfaction with the quality and services provided by local Hong Kong tour guides. Zhang and Chow (2004) applied the importance-performance analysis (IPA) technique to investigate the performance of Hong Kong tour guides as perceived by mainland Chinese inbound tourists to Hong Kong. Huang (2010a) applied a revised IPA analysis to evaluate the performance of tour guides in Shanghai. Chan (2004) investigated the effect of tour services on customer satisfaction in package tours in Hong Kong and identified that tourist satisfaction with tour service was largely determined by tour guide service.

While theoretical development in the tour guiding research is generally weak (Weiler & Kim, 2011), some studies examining the causal relationship between tour guiding performance and tourist satisfaction did attempt to develop and test theory. Of particular note is Huang *et al.*'s (2010) study that tested a multilayer framework of tourist satisfaction in the package tour context. The study found that tour guide performance had a significant effect on tourist satisfaction with the guiding service and an indirect effect on satisfaction with the tour service and the tour experience. Satisfaction with the guiding service positively affected satisfaction with the tour service but showed no direct effect on satisfaction with the overall tour experience. Recently, Huang *et al.* (2015) investigated the effects of both cognitive and affective tour guide interpretation outcome on mainland Chinese visitors' satisfaction and behavioural intention in a heritage tourist attraction in Australia. They found that cognitive interpretation outcome had a greater impact on tourist satisfaction and sustaining visitor arrivals than affective interpretation outcome, whereas satisfaction with the guided tour experience directly affects behavioural intention and largely mediated the effect of cognitive interpretation outcome on behavioural intention.

Tour guide training and education is key to improving guiding performance. In most cases, lack of training leads to multi-faceted consequences on visitors, tour operators and tour guides themselves. These include poor guiding performance, unethical guiding practice, low guide self-esteem, job burnout and damage to the destination image (Weiler & Black, 2015). More often, guide training is associated with the quality assurance or qualification certification of tour guiding (Black & Weiler, 2005; Huang & Weiler, 2010). In relation to professional certification, other issues explored in the literature include licensing, codes of conduct, professional associations and professional awards of excellence in tour guiding (Huang & Weiler, 2010; Weiler & Black, 2015). All these issues seem to be quite practical and subject to specific regulations in different countries (Black & Weiler, 2005; Huang & Weiler, 2010; Mak *et al.*, 2009, 2011).

Tour Guide and Interpretation Research in China

In China, tour guiding is a highly regulated practice. In 1987, the China National Tourism Administration (CNTA) issued the *Provisional Measures on Tour Guides Administration*, starting the official regulation and administration on tour guides (Huang & Weiler, 2010). Together with these provisional administration measures on tour guides, two years later, CNTA launched the National Tour Guide Qualification Examination (NTGQE) for guide qualification certification and a tour guide licensing and registration system (Huang & Weiler, 2010). In 1999, the State Council of the People's Republic of China promulgated the *Administrative Regulations on Tour Guides*, replacing the previous *Provisional Measures*. So far, the *Administrative Regulations on Tour Guides* remains one of the only three state-level administrative acts promulgated by the State Council, the other two being the *Administrative Measures on Chinese Citizens' Outbound Travel* promulgated in 2001 and the *Travel Agency Act* most recently revised and re-issued in 2009 (Huang, 2010b). It should be noted that, to a certain extent, the other two state-level administrative acts would also indirectly regulate tour guiding.

The nature of the highly regulated tour guiding practice in China had not been widely acknowledged outside China in the English tourism literature until Huang and Weiler's (2010) work was published. Huang and Weiler (2010) provided a comprehensive critical review on China tour guiding quality assurance systems covering various relevant issues ranging from tour guide qualification examinations, certification, licensing, the classification of different levels of guides and training, to awards of guiding excellence, professional associations and codes of ethics. This article provides a panoramic view for outside researchers and practitioners to understand the tour guide administration system in China. Other studies in relation to tour guides and guiding in China, mostly conducted by Huang and his colleagues (e.g. Huang, 2010a, 2010b, 2015) were mainly around tour guiding performance, service quality and package tourist satisfaction and behaviours (Weiler & Black, 2015).

Despite these relevant studies published in English tourism journals, much of the tour guiding and interpretation in China remains blind to researchers outside China. In this section, we provide a dedicated review of tour guides and interpretation research in China. Consistent with other chapters in this book, our review covers four leading Chinese tourism journals, *Tourism Tribune*, *Tourism Science*, *Human Geography* and *Economic Geography*, for the period from 2006 to 2013.

Tour Guiding Service Quality and Quality Assurance

A variety of topics have been identified on improving China's tour guiding quality assurance system. These include tour guide administration and certification systems (Liu, 2011; Song & Wang, 2013); guiding service quality (Liu, 2009; Wang & Ma, 2007; Xie & Li); and the remuneration of tour guides (Li, 2007; Xu & Jiang, 2006). In most cases, the discussion scope of these articles is broad and the discussions overlap across different articles. Like most articles identified by Huang and Hsu (2008) as qualitative articles following an essay format, these articles lack clearly stated methods and are mostly opinion pieces with critical logic reasoning and analysis. In China's tourism administration, tour guide management and its administration issues are central issues concerning both the government and industry. Researchers in China tend to pick up administrative issues in their studies (Xie, 2003). With regard to tour guide administration and certification systems, many researchers have criticised the current policy system on certification and licensing and recommended various policy considerations with the aim of improving the system. The low education entry level in tour guide qualification examination (any high school graduate can take the exam and be licensed as a tour guide) has been frequently mentioned as one of the weaknesses in the system (e.g. Liu, 2011; Song & Wang, 2013). By the end of 2010, the total number of licensed tour guides in China was around 600,000, while in 2004 there were only 195,000 licensed tour guides (Liu, 2011). Liu (2011) noted that over 80% of the 600,000 licensed tour guides were only educated at junior college level or below. Many of the currently practising tour guides in China are believed to lack sufficient knowledge to take a guiding job. Among Chinese scholars, there seem to be many voices and debates around the tour guide certification system. Song and Wang (2013) argue that the tour guide certification and licensing system in China plays a very limited role in curbing the market opportunism problems in the industry (that is, unlicensed guides provide low-quality service), controlling the number of tour guides and improving guiding service quality. Instead, they believe an industry governance model focused on travel agencies as the core responsible entity should be considered for a better system design. Li and Wang (2009) take a so-called 'legal-economics' perspective in critiquing the current certification and licensing system. They argue that in the current industry situation tour guides have low job satisfaction, high turnover to other professions, and the low quality of the tour guide workforce as well as the general low service quality in tour guiding cannot be resolved by simply reforming the tour guide remuneration system; instead, the tour guide certification system as the gateway to the profession should be reformed to balance the supply of tour guides and tour guiding service quality.

Along China's institutional evolution towards a market economy, travel companies and tour operators tend not to employ tour guides as their internal employees, but instead hire licensed tour guides on a temporary and casual basis under the administration system. To adapt to this market change, tourism administrations establish agencies that manage tour guides in different regions. Most of these agencies are known as either 'tour guide service corporations' or 'tour guide service centres' and are registered to take over some of the administrative responsibilities of tourism authorities such as guide licensing registration, annual auditing, and routine administrative training. As self-financed organisations, they charge management fees to tour guides who are affiliated with them and introduce them to guiding jobs assigned by tour operators, and in turn, take a commission as an intermediary between the guide and the tour operator. It is estimated that over 80% of the entire tour guide workforce may have non-permanent employment status in affiliation with these tour guide service corporations, making tour guiding a highly unstable profession in China (Liu, 2011). The tour guides accepting such employment status are often referred to as 'social tour guides', compared to the small number of so-called fully employed tour guides who are formal permanent employees of travel agency companies.

With such an 'informally' employed tour guiding workforce, service quality is of great concern. Wang and Ma (2007), based on the national domestic tourist survey results, noted that the tour guiding service was perceived by tourist consumers as among the poorest service items. This may be interpreted as a serious industry problem if you bear in mind that other researchers like Xie and Li (2007) used empirical surveys to prove that perceived tour guiding service and tourist satisfaction with tour guiding affected tourist intentions to recommend and continue to use the same travel company. Other researchers such as Liu (2009) applied the stakeholder theory in seeking the reasons for the unsatisfactory tour guiding service prevalent in the tourism industry. Liu (2009) argues that imbalanced interests and the power structure among the key tourism stakeholders has caused the current low guiding service quality problem.

It has been a long-established industry practice in China that tour guides do not usually get paid by the tour operators who contract the guiding service tasks to them. More often, tour operators compete with low prices to attract customers, and this reduced cost pressure is passed on to the tour guides. Most tour guides have to pay back a 'head-count fee' according to the number of tourists in the received tour group and are forced to live on shopping commissions as their labour return (Huang, 2010b; Liu, 2009). Liu (2009) argued that the imbalanced power and interest structure and relations among the stakeholders should be blamed for causing the current guiding service problems rather than the tour guides themselves. Such an empathetic view towards tour guides has been shared by other scholars. For example, Chen (2006) condemned the fact that the vocational rights of tour guides have long been overlooked in the current industry management and administration system. First, tour guides' licensed job rights have been infringed by other people such as tour managers, interns and tour bus drivers in the industry and within the tour companies; secondly, tour guides' job payment and deserved social welfare rights are not guaranteed; and thirdly, tour guides' rights to receive professional training cannot be effectively maintained. Chen (2006) argued that multiple parties including the government, tour guide associations, unions and tour companies should work together to improve the channels representing tour guides' interests.

Many scholars have noted that the remuneration system for tour guiding, as it is currently practised, harms the tour guide profession and partially causes the service quality problems. As such, many researchers have attempted to seek measures to reform the current tour guide remuneration system. Li and Wang (2009) summarised four specific approaches to reforming the current system: the first approach recommends balanced interest sharing between the tour operator and the tour guide by increasing the fixed income of tour guides through the tour operator's direct payment; the second advocates an open and fair mechanism that clarifies tour guides' salary return and commission earned by acknowledging the legitimacy of commission income and appropriate economic relationships among tour operators, local tourist service providers (e.g. hotels, theme parks) and the tour guide; the third approach argues for a legal commission system by reforming the current commission rebate practice and commission ratio; and the fourth approach suggests legalising the tour guiding tipping system to increase tour guide earnings.

In addition to seeking administrative remedies to deal with the tour guide remuneration issues, some scholars aimed to develop an ideal tour guide payment system directly. For instance, Xu and Jiang (2006) worked to construct a comprehensive tour guide remuneration index system which considers labour cost, intellectual and physical inputs, and performance-based incentives (penalties). The system consists of three levels of indicators with varying weightings. On the other hand, Li (2007) applied the psychological contract theory and analysed the tour guiding service tipping system. It should be noted that tipping the tour guiding service is still a controversial issue in China. While the CNTA has made it quite clear that any type of explicit or implicit request for tips from tour guides to their clients is prohibited, the industry has seen ramifications in tipping practice to tour guides. In 2004, The Guangdong China Travel Service Company introduced the Western-style tipping system into its tour guide remuneration system and ignited quite some discussion and industry debates on the issue (Li, 2007; Li & Wang, 2009). Drawing upon the psychological contract theory, Li (2007) argues that the uncertainty of the psychological contract between tourists and tour guides determines the uncertainty of tourist tipping to tour guides; right now the tourism industry environment is not suitable for tipping practice in tour guiding, and for the time being tipping may only apply to upscale 'pure recreation' (no shopping) package tours.

Tour Guide Behaviour

It should be noted that a small number of studies have investigated tour guide behaviour. These include tour guide ethical behaviour (He *et al.*, 2010; Wu, 2010), job satisfaction (Tian & Pu, 2006), and emotional labour (Yan *et al.*, 2012). Most of these studies take a quantitative approach. For instance, Wu (2010) proposed a multidimensional construct for tour guide ethical behaviour and used survey data to confirm that tour guide ethical behaviour includes four dimensions: preserving a professional image; proper guiding and assistance in tourist shopping; ensuring service quality; and law-abiding behaviour. Wu (2010) also applied structural equation modelling analysis and found that an organisational ethical climate had positive effects on the ethical behaviour dimensions, while job outcome oriented control negatively affected two ethical behaviour dimensions: proper guiding and assistance in tourist shopping, and law-abiding behaviours. Applying the dynamic optimisation method in economics, He *et al.* (2010) developed a model rationalising tour guides' unethical behaviour, noting that income from ethical practice, government monitoring and penalty severity are three major influencing factors for managing tour guides' risk-taking behaviours to engage in unethical guiding practice.

Building on the practical concerns about low job satisfaction among tour guides in China and the high rate of tour guides leaving the profession, Tian and Pu (2006) tested the relationship of various possible factors and tour guides' job satisfaction. The study identified that social evaluation and general attitudes toward tour guides significantly affected tour guides' job satisfaction; personal career development prospects, together with job satisfaction, affected tour guides' loyalty to the profession and turnover intentions. Job safety and security were also found to be important in affecting tour guides' job satisfaction and job loyalty.

Yan *et al.*'s (2012) study is one of the few studies exploring tour guides' emotional labour in the Chinese context. Studying Chinese tour guides in East China, the authors found that tour guides' emotional labour involvement positively affected their emotional exhaustion, while emotional exhaustion negatively affected their job satisfaction. While surface acting was found to positively affect emotional exhaustion, deep acting, through self-adjustment and internalising job responsibilities and demands, helped effectively reduce the level of emotional exhaustion.

Legal Relations Regarding Tour Guides in China

Tour guiding is a licensed profession in China, like other professions such as lawyers and accountants. However, unlike these other professions which require substantial specialised skills and knowledge, the entry level for tour guiding is relatively low. In the transitional economy of China, tour guiding as a profession is also closely related to the tourism industry governance which takes travel agency management and the market (dis)order issues at its core (Song & Wang, 2013). With the implementation of China's new Labour Law in 2008, the legal relations facing tour guides in China become more complicated (Wang, 2008, 2009). Wang (2008, 2009) ran some in-depth analysis to clarify the legal relationship. Wang's (2008, 2009) argument is based on the differentiation of two interrelated legal concepts: labour relations (*Laodong guanxi*) and labour service relations (*laowu guanxi*). Labour relations (*Laodong guanxi*) are defined as the relationship between an employer and its employees and the related legal rights and obligations/ responsibilities. Labour service relations happen when two civil parties reach an agreement over the transaction of one party's labour service to another with a market price. In China's current industry circumstances, most of the 'social' tour guides are working on a *de facto* self-employment basis. Even though they have to be affiliated to a tour guide management corporation to fulfil professional management requirements (e.g. licensing, annual training and work auditing) imposed by the tourism authorities, the tour guide management corporations cannot be their employer in the legal sense. Generally, the corporation is not obliged to pay the affiliated tour guides' salaries; nor is it obliged to fulfil other legal obligations like paying social insurance for the guides as prescribed by the Labour Law to an employer. As tour guides mostly work for tour operators or travel agencies on a contractual basis, the relationship between the guide, his/her management corporation, and the travel agency contracting the guiding service work become complicated. Wang (2009) criticised a case in which the justice authorities regarded the relationship between a tour guide and the affiliated tour guide management corporation as a labour relationship between an employee and an employer. Wang argues that, following this understanding of the legal relationship between a tour guide and the affiliated management corporation, the legal procedures are unduly cumbersome and tour guides' rights cannot be effectively protected. Instead, clarifying the legal relationship between the tour guide and the travel agency assigning tour service tasks as labour service relations and that between the tour guide and the tour guide management corporation as intermediation service relations would resolve any legal disputes and issues more effectively (Wang, 2009).

Interpretation Research in China

Interpretation research in China has been at an early development stage. Most studies have focused on the construction of a comprehensive interpretation system with little theory testing and building effort (Wu *et al.*, 1999;

Zhong, 1999; Zhu, 2011). Zhu (2011) searched the relevant databases in China and found 153 articles relating to tourist and environmental interpretation and 49 articles pertaining to visitor education and environmental education up to July 2009. The themes of these articles could be identified as being in four areas: (1) meaning and significance of interpretation; (2) classification and construction of the interpretation content and system; (3) interpretation and visitor education planning steps and procedures; and (4) planning and design of an interpretation system.

Our review of the relevant articles in interpretation in the four Chinese tourist journals did not reveal anything substantially different from what Zhu (2011) describes as the current state of interpretation research in China. Generally, interpretation has been acknowledged as an important factor in visitor education and natural heritage protection (Tao et al., 2009; Wei, 2010; Zhu, 2011). Following early studies (Wu et al., 1999; Zhong, 1999), researchers are still seeking to conceptually construct the system of interpretation in tourist attractions. For instance, Tang (2006) presents a conceptual framework of tourist attraction interpretation which includes the object of the recognition (information source), the user (receiver) and tourism interpretation (communication media). Focusing on the self-guided interpretation system (versus personal guiding interpretation; see Wu et al., 1999), Tang (2006) constructed the media means of a self-guided interpretation system as onsite signage, offsite virtual presentation (visitor centre), and detachable media (printings, audio-video products).

In conceptualising the interpretation system, most research tends to describe the subsystems, components and associated functions of the interpretation system. Critiquing on the atheoretical nature of such research, Zhang (2011) introduced the means–end value chain theory to underlie the construction of interpretive systems. Zhang (2011) argues that any interpretation system is in essence an information exchange system, and the ultimate purpose of an interpretation system is to enable interaction between the tourist attraction and the tourist, realise the tourist's value and needs, and eventually seek the maximisation of the attraction's economic, social and ecological benefits. Through identifying the means–end value chain, different effective interpretation systems can be designed to meet the needs of different tourists (e.g. independent travellers, hiking tourists and leisure tourists).

While many studies evaluated the needs of establishing an interpretation system from the supply perspective, recently researchers in China started to investigate the visitor needs in the interpretation system (Gan & Lu, 2012; Hong & Tao, 2006; Luo et al., 2008; Zhang et al., 2010). These studies were conducted in different types of tourist attractions, including museums (Gan

& Lu, 2012; Hong & Tao, 2006); national geological parks (Zhang *et al.*, 2010), and world natural heritage sites (Luo *et al.*, 2008). Personal guiding interpretation was identified as the preferred interpretation means across these studies (cf. Gan & Lu, 2012; Luo *et al.*, 2008; Zhang *et al.*, 2010). Tourists' preferences for different ways of interpretation and some behavioural needs (motivations, expectations) were generally cross-examined with socio-demographic variables. However, the generalisability of the findings is limited due to the highly contextualised nature of the studies.

Interpretation research in China tends to focus on the non-personal interpretation means and the construction of such non-personal interpretation systems. Interpretation research has been directed by the needs of the tourist attraction development and thus has taken an industry supply perspective to treat interpretation as a major management design in specific attraction planning. There still seems to be a big gap in understanding the personal guide interpretation in tourist attractions. Attraction-based tour guides face different job requirements in China; they need more localised knowledge and skills and lean more towards interpretation in their job roles. Although attraction-based tour guiding interpretation has been examined in relation to visitor outcomes (attitudinal and behavioural) in a Chinese context outside China (see Huang *et al.*, 2015), virtually no research has been done to look into interpretive guiding (personal interpretation) and how interpretive guiding affects tourist satisfaction in China.

Conclusion

This chapter reviews the tour guiding and interpretation research in China. The review has been conducted through a comparative lens with reference to the tour guiding research as summarised by Weiler and Black (2015). The chapter reveals that the tour guiding research in China is mainly focused on tour guide management issues, such as professional certification, tour guide remuneration and tipping. A small number of studies investigated tour guide behaviour in various contexts, such as ethical guiding behaviours and the legal relations that tour guides face in China. It can be concluded that practical government and industry concerns have largely guided the tour guiding research in China. The highly regulated context of tour guiding in China, together with the market situation in China's transitional economy, may have formed the pathway for tour guiding research in China. Therefore, the difference of tour guiding research in and outside China can be better explained by referring to the country's industry and regulative environment towards tour guiding.

While tour guiding research has mostly taken an administrative perspective, interpretation research has mostly followed the industry supply perspective. Understandably, constructing an effective interpretation system within tourist attractions dominates the interpretation research currently taking place in China. Most of the interpretation research belongs to the domain of attraction management planning. Very little research has been directed to the personal interpretation services delivered by attraction-based tour guides.

As noted by Weiler and Black (2015), theoretical development in tour guiding research in the English literature has been weak. Similarly, both tour guiding and interpretation research in China have been weak in terms of theory building and testing. Unlike what is demonstrated in the English literature, although tour guides serve as important frontline contact staff in the tourism industry, little research has been conducted in China to examine the relationship between tour guiding performance, service quality and tourists' behavioural responses. It is speculated that guide–tourist interaction is an unexplored area in tourism studies that may enrich both tourist behaviour and tour guiding research. And it is also an area in which relevant theories such as the intergroup contact theory, social exchange theory and social representation theory can be further tested and developed in tour guiding research. As such, tour guiding and interpretation research in China, like that outside China, needs more theorising and contextualised theory testing in the future.

References

Black, R. (2002) Toward a model of tour guide certification: An analysis of the Australia Ecoguide Program. Unpublished doctoral dissertation, Monash University, Melbourne, Australia.

Black, R. and Weiler, B. (eds) (2003) *Interpreting the Land Down Under: Australian Heritage Interpretation and Tour Guiding*. Boulder, CO: Fulcrum.

Black, R. and Weiler, B. (2005) Quality assurance and regulatory mechanisms in the tour guiding industry: A systematic review. *Journal of Tourism Studies* 16 (1), 24–37.

Chan, A. (2004) Towards an improved understanding of tour services and customer satisfaction in package tours. Paper presented at the Second Asia-Pacific CHRIE Conference and Sixth Biennial Conference on Tourism in Asia, Phuket, Thailand.

Chen, T. (2006) On safeguarding the professional rights and interests of tour guides and their benefit expression. *Tourism Tribune* 21 (4), 60–66.

Cohen, E. (1985) The tourist guide: The origins, structure and dynamics of a role. *Annals of Tourism Research* 12 (1), 5–29.

Cohen, E.H., Ifergan, M. and Cohen, E. (2002) A new paradigm in guiding: The *Madrich* as a role model. *Annals of Tourism Research* 29 (4), 919–932.

Dahles, H. (2002) The politics of tour guiding: Image management in Indonesia. *Annals of Tourism Research* 29 (3), 738–800.

Dong, L.C., Droege, S.B. and Johnson, N.B. (2002) Incentives and self-interest: Balancing revenue and rewards in China's tourism industry. *Tourism and Hospitality Research* 4, 69–77.

Gan, L. and Lu, T. (2012) Study on visitors' expectations, use and evaluation of museum interpretation systems: An analysis based on knowledge needs. *Tourism Tribune* 27 (9), 56–64.

Geva, A. and Goldman, A. (1991) Satisfaction measurement in guided tours. *Annals of Tourism Research* 18 (2), 177–185.

Ham, S.H. (1992) *Environmental Interpretation: A Practical Guide for People with Big Ideas and Small Budgets*. Golden, CO: North American Press.

He, A., Xiao, Z. and Liu, S. (2010) An analysis of tour guides' moral risks based on dynamic optimization model. *Tourism Tribune* 25 (9), 65–70.

Hong, Y. and Tao, W. (2006) Tourists' demands for interpretative media: A case study of the museum of the mausoleum of the Nanyue King. *Tourism Tribune* 21 (11), 43–48.

Hu, W. and Wall, G. (2012) Interpretive guiding and sustainable development: A framework. *Tourism Management Perspectives* 4, 80–85.

Huang, S. (2010a) A revised importance-performance analysis of tour guide performance in China. *Tourism Analysis* 15 (2), 227–241.

Huang, S. (2010b) Toward a behavioral theory of government–firm relationship behavior: 'thick-description' of the dynamics of government's role in shaping China's domestic, inbound, and outbound tourism industry. In A. Woodside (ed.) *Advances in Culture, Tourism and Hospitality Research*, Vol. 4 (pp. 149–163). Bingley: Emerald.

Huang, S. (2015) Tour guide. In J. Jafari and H. Xiao (eds) *Encyclopedia of Tourism*. New York: Springer.

Huang, S. and Hsu, C.H.C. (2008) Recent tourism and hospitality research in China. *International Journal of Hospitality & Tourism Administration* 9 (3), 267–287.

Huang, S. and Weiler, B. (2010) A review and evaluation of China's quality assurance system for tour guiding. *Journal of Sustainable Tourism* 18 (7), 845–860.

Huang, S., Hsu, C.H.C. and Chan, A. (2010) Tour guide performance and tourist satisfaction: A study of the package tours in Shanghai. *Journal of Hospitality and Tourism Research* 34 (1), 3–33.

Huang, S., Weiler, B. and Assaker, G. (2015) Effects of interpretive guiding outcomes on tourist satisfaction and behavioural intention. *Journal of Travel Research* 54 (3), 344–358; doi:10.1177/0047287513517426.

Katz, S. (1985) The Israeli teacher-guide: The emergence and perpetuation of a role. *Annals of Tourism Research* 12, 49–72.

Li, J. (2007) Psychology contract and tour guide tip system. *Tourism Tribune* 22 (9), 41–44.

Li, X. and Wang, B. (2009) Study on the solution of practising crisis of China's domestic tour guides under the perspective of legal economics. *Tourism Tribune* 24 (9), 73–78.

Liu, A. (2011) Discussion about making strict demands on the access system of tour guides and improving the management system of tour guides. *Tourism Tribune* 26 (5), 62–67.

Liu, H. (2009) An analysis of the source of problems regarding tour guide service quality and study for countermeasures – based on stakeholder theory and visitors' perspective visual angle. *Tourism Tribune* 24 (1), 37–41.

Luo, F., Zhong, Y., Wu, Z. and Zhang, X. (2008) Tourism interpretive demand of visitors in World Natural Heritage Site – take Wulingyuan as an example. *Tourism Tribune* 23 (8), 69–73.

Mak, A.H.N., Wong, K.K.F. and Chang, R.C.Y. (2009) Factors affecting the service quality of the tour guiding profession in Macau. *International Journal of Tourism Research* 12 (3), 205–218.

Mak, A.H.N., Wong, K.K.F. and Chang, R.C.Y. (2011) Critical issues affecting the service quality and professionalism of the tour guides in Hong Kong and Macau. *Tourism Management* 32 (6), 1442–1452.

Mossberg, L.L. (1995) Tour leaders and their importance in charter tours. *Tourism Management* 16 (6), 437–445.

Quality of Tour Guide Service (1995) *Quality of tour guide service 9GB/T 15971 – 1995).* Retrieved on January 29, 2008 from http://www.cnta.gov.cn/news_detail/newsshow.asp?id=A20066231654396087959

Skibins, J.C., Powell, R.B. and Stern, M.J. (2012) Exploring empirical support for interpretation's best practices. *Journal of Interpretation Research* 17 (1), 25–44.

Song, Z. and Wang, Y. (2013) Analysis of the access system and management of tour guides. *Tourism Tribune* 28 (7), 57–63.

Tang, M. (2006) A framework for interpretation system in tourist areas. *Tourism Tribune* 21 (1), 64–68.

Tao, W., Du, X. and Hong, Y. (2009) Interpretation: An important tactics for heritage conservation. *Tourism Tribune* 24 (8), 47–52.

Tian, X. and Pu, Y. (2006) An analysis of the job satisfaction of tour guiding and its empirical evaluation. *Tourism Tribune* 21 (6), 91–95.

Tilden, F. (1977) *Interpreting Our Heritage* (3rd edn).Chapel Hill, NC: North Carolina Press.

Wang C. (2008) Influences of Labour Contract Law on the legal relations between tour guides and their employers. *Tourism Science* 22 (5), 74–78.

Wang C. (2009) On the expurgation of legal relations between part-time tour guides, tour guide service companies and travel agencies. *Tourism Tribune* 24 (11), 64–70.

Wang, J. and Ma, Y. (2007) New visual angle of improving the quality of guide services – concurrently a review of guide service management and research in the past 20 years. *Tourism Tribune* 22 (3), 64–70.

Wei, D. (2010) Environmental interpretation evaluation: A literature review. *Tourism Science* 24 (5), 84–94.

Weiler, B. and Black, R. (2015) *Tour Guiding Research: Insights, Issues and Implications.* Bristol: Channel View Publications.

Weiler, B. and Kim, A.K. (2011) Tour guides as agents of sustainability: Rhetoric, reality and implications for research. *Tourism Recreation Research* 36 (2), 113–125.

Weiler, B. and Yu, X. (2007) Dimensions of cultural mediation in guiding Chinese tour groups: Implications for interpretation. *Tourism Recreation Research* 32 (3), 13–22.

Wong, A. (2001) Satisfaction with local tour guides in Hong Kong. *Pacific Tourism Review* 5 (1), 59–67.

World Federation of Tourist Guide Associations (WFTGA) (2003) What is a tourist guide? Retrieved on June 16, 2005 from http://www.wftga.org.page.asp?id=15

Wu, B., Jing, L. and Zhang, L. (1999) Study on tour guiding interpretation system – the case of Beijing. *Human Geography* 2, 27–29.

Wu, X. (2010) Professional ethical behaviour of tour guides: Structural composition and influencing reasons. *Tourism Tribune* 24 (6), 28–38,

Xie, L. and Li, J. (2007) A study of the relationships between tour guides' service quality and tourists' trust and behavioural intentions. *Tourism Science* 21 (4), 43–48.

Xie, Y. (2003) Tourism and hospitality industry studies: A comparative research between China and the overseas countries. *Tourism Tribune* 18 (5), 20–25.

Xu, H., Cui, Q., Ballantyne, R. and Packer, J. (2013) Effective environmental interpretation at Chinese natural attractions: The need for an aesthetic approach. *Journal of Sustainable Tourism* 21 (1), 117–133.

Xu, L. and Jiang, K. (2006) A research on the index system of tour guide salary. *Tourism Science* 20 (6), 71–76.

Yan, Q., Wu, Y., Yang, Y. and Kong, H. (2012) An exploration of emotional labor of tour guides in East China Itinerary and its empirical enlightenment – application of structural equation model (SEM). *Tourism Tribune* 27 (3), 78–83.

Yu, X., Weiler, B. and Ham, S. (2002) Intercultural communication and mediation: A framework of analysing intercultural competence of Chinese tour guides. *Journal of Vacation Marketing* 8 (1), 75–87.

Zhang, B. (2011) Construction of the humanism tour interpretive services system based on means–end theory. *Human Geography* 5, 143–147.

Zhang, H.Q. and Chow, I. (2004) Application of importance-performance model in tour guides' performance: Evidence from mainland Chinese outbound visitors in Hong Kong. *Tourism Management* 25 (1), 81–91.

Zhong, L. (1999) On the education of ecological tourists. *Sixiang Zhanxian* 6, 39–42.

Zhang, L., Wu, C., Peng, Y. and Zhao, H. (2010) Research on interpretation demand at geological relics sights: A case study of Cuihuashan National Geo-park in Shaanxi Province. *Tourism Science* 24 (6), 39–46.

Zhu, X. (2011) Literature review on environment interpretation and visitor education in China. *Tourism Science* 25 (2), 85–94.

8 Tourism Research in China: Concluding Remarks

Introduction

This book offers a selective review of the tourism research terrain in China. The review covers some key research topics including Chinese scholars' epistemological views of tourism, rural tourism, community participation in tourism, tourist markets and behaviour, tourist attraction management, and tour guiding and interpretation in China. It is not our intention to review all the important tourism research topics in China. The selection of these topics is largely determined by the research interests and expertise of the two authors and their continuing observations on the industry's development in relation to the topics. This chapter provides some concluding remarks on tourism research in China. Specifically, we focus on a few distinct issues that may help researchers outside China to better understand the tourism research scenarios in China. In the following discussions, we try to refer back to the previous chapters to highlight the issues being discussed.

The Role of Government and Power Relations in Tourism Development

China has been implementing a government-led tourism development strategy (Kuang, 2001). The government plays a significant role in tourism development in China. In examining tourism development models and especially community involvement in tourism development in China, the government should always be treated as a significant actor. In Chapter 4, we discussed the different models of community participation and involvement in tourism. To better understand the cases presented in the chapter, one must have a sufficient level of knowledge about the political environment in China. Unlike most Western countries, China has a more powerful government which can mobilise the necessary social, political and economic resources to achieve its goals. The 2008 Olympic Games is one example which shows the Chinese government's capacity for social mobilisation. Bearing this in mind, it is not surprising to find that, in most community-involved tourism development cases, the government is a more powerful stakeholder than any other actor.

It is also important to note that in China's government system, the central government has differing interests and goals from those of local governments (provincial and sub-provincial level governments). While the central government may be more concerned with China's overall economic and social development, local governments tend to be more bound to the interests of generating fiscal revenues from local economic development and are more concerned with their gross domestic product (GDP) growth. Clearly, local governments should be differentiated from the central government in China in their interests and involvement in tourism. In the limited English publications talking about Chinese government roles in tourism, there is a lack of such differentiation. Researchers outside China are therefore reminded of such a distinction between the central government and local governments in China in their respective roles in China tourism development.

In most of the community-based tourism cases presented in Chapter 4 and the attraction management issues in Chapter 6, local government plays a dominant role in directing tourism development. In some cases, the local government's roles and interests intertwine with those of tourism investors and development companies. It is not unusual to see local government as the headmaster of tourism enterprises involved in the community tourism development. Such an intimate relationship between local government and tourism investment/development companies would be a significant factor influencing the outcome of community-based tourism development in China. Such an asymmetric power relationship between government/tourism companies and local residents would not favour a sustainable community involvement model without social tension and conflicts.

Admittedly, Chinese society is changing and accordingly the power structure and relationships among government, tourism enterprises, community (and tourists) will be transformed. Of special note are the influences of the internet and the development of netizenship in China. Under such influences, it is easier for community members to express their concerns about the tourism development cases they are involved in and to attract media attention. Generally speaking, local residents are increasingly aware of their rights and would like to protect their rights in any type of tourism development that affects their own lives.

Although there seems to be increasing rights awareness among community members in community-based tourism cases, as demonstrated in many of such cases, local residents are more concerned with benefit sharing in tourism development than participating in decision-making. This may be due to the rooted culture of Chinese rural society. It has been noted by some scholars (e.g. Lin, 1936) that in Chinese rural villages, there is a lack of civil society citizenship and the corresponding governance structure. This offers reasonable explanations as to why most local residents are more concerned with benefit sharing than decision-making as well as the elite governance model in some cases. In China, there is a long tradition of 'government by gentleman' and in villages clan elders and elites are often the *de facto* adjudicators and decision-makers in respect of various issues (Lin, 1936).

Despite the above cultural explanations, from a rational and scientific perspective, Chinese tourism researchers would like to see a more sustainable community involvement model that enables a higher level of involvement of local residents in decision-making. This has been indicated in Chapter 4. However, how applicable a democratic decision-making mechanism is in community-based tourism development in China is subject to further empirical verification. Community empowerment may be one way to achieve this but when applying this concept in the Chinese context, one should bear in mind the cultural differences and fabrications in the new context.

Research Institutions and their Influence on Tourism Research

Tourism researchers in China tend to be less critical and reflexive about their research practices than their international counterparts. While it is not unusual to see tourism researchers in the international tourism academy adopting highly reflexive research approaches and methodologies such as the critical theory approach and autoethnography (e.g. Botterill, 2003; Hall, 2004; Tribe, 2001, 2006; Wearing & Wearing, 2001), researchers in China seldom reflect on the researcher's self in the research process and the research institution. This may be partly due to the education system, research culture and research institutions in China. From our observations, we note that critical thinking and critical review and evaluation of the literature have not been fully evidenced in Chinese journal articles. As noted by Tribe (2006), ideology serves as one important factor that influences research and knowledge production. Of course, there still exists an entrenched ideological difference between China and the Western world. Therefore, the prevailing research paradigms and approaches taken by tourism researchers in China may be a result of the dominant ideologies in the country. Chapters 1 and 2 of this book alluded to the institutional and ideological influences in tourism research in China. Researchers outside China who have collaborative contact with co-researchers in China may have first-hand experience of how ideologies affect Chinese researchers' research practices. Ironically, even though critical theory as a research paradigm is greatly informed by Marxist ideology (Tribe, 2006), in the current political climate in China, it is unlikely that critical theory can be adopted by many researchers in China.

Chinese Laws and Tourism

On 25 April 2013, the People's Congress Standing Committee of China passed the Tourism Law, which has been effective since 1 October 2013. As stated in the first clause of the Law, the purpose of making this legislation is to protect the legal rights of both tourists and tourism business operators, to regulate the tourism market, and to order, protect and appropriately utilise tourism resources in order to ensure continuous and healthy development of the tourism industry. In China's legislation system, such a national law, as passed by the legislative body of the People's Congress and issued by the President of China, represents the intention of the State to see tourism as a strategically important industry in the country. This is in line with the government-led tourism development strategy and the strong governmental power and role in China's tourism development as discussed elsewhere in this book.

There have been discussions among tourism academics and industry practitioners on the implications of the Tourism Law over the past two years. However, it was not our intention to review these discussions as most of them are opinion pieces and lack the rigour and depth of research work. To better understand various issues in China's tourism development, another two laws seem to be relevant and need to be discussed.

The first law is the law of land management. Defined by China's socialist system, land in China cannot be *owned* as private property. The Land Administration Law of China clearly states that 'The People's Republic of China enacts a socialist public ownership on land, that is, ownership by the whole people and collective ownership by the working people' (Clause 2, Land Administration Law, available at http://www.china.com.cn/chinese/law/647616.htm). Such land ownership prescribed by law in China defines some distinct features of China's tourism development. In understanding most of the practical issues included in Chapter 3 with regard to rural tourism and in Chapter 4 for community participation and involvement in tourism, the land ownership system in China ultimately explains the relationships of the stakeholders in tourism development and the many issues and conflicts centred around land use and land use/development rights among government, enterprises and communities. The law puts the government as the representative of the State to be the land 'owner' and manager in effect; this, together with the authoritarian administration system in China, further puts the community in a weakened position in dealing with any land use issues in tourism. When examining various rural tourism and community tourism issues in China, the land ownership system should be taken as an important reference.

The second law is the Labour Law. As mentioned in Chapter 7 in relation to the 'social' tour guides management issue, the interpretation and application of the Labour Law has significant implications in accommodating and resolving many practical labour relations disputes and issues in the current tour guides administration system in China. As a profession, tour guides have been subject to strict government regulation in China. However, the nature of tour guiding in the industry and the labour relations structure of tour guides in the tourism services provision positions tour guiding as a very complicated industry problem. It seems clarifying the labour relations referring to the Labour Law may contribute to a better system in regulating tour guiding in China.

Tourist Behaviour Research: Awaiting More Academic Attention and Theoretical Advancements

It has been acknowledged that tourism research in China focuses more on industry supply and macro-management issues than demand-side issues. This may be explained by the government's effort in developing the infrastructural and product supplies in tourism in the past three decades. Having said this, we must note that there is a trend for both the government and the tourism academy in China to attend more to tourists as consumers and citizens in the future. In February 2013, the State Council published the *National Tourism and Leisure Guidelines* in China. This implies that the tourism administration will not only focus on industry management, but also take on the social and welfare issues of Chinese nationals. The recent promulgation of the Tourism Law in China reinforced the tourist rights issues in the consumer society. We foresee that all these changes will lead to more consumer research in relation to tourism. The leisure needs of Chinese nationals will be disclosed in further research following the government lead; the contribution of tourism and leisure to individual well-being and social welfare will also be investigated and acknowledged in tourism research in China. In relation to our evaluation of the tourist market and behaviour research in China in Chapter 5, we also expect that, with an increasing number of tourist behaviour studies, it is likely that we will see good theoretical contributions coming out of this line of research in China.

References

Botterill, D. (2003) An autoethnographic narrative on tourism research epistemologies. *Society and Leisure* 26 (1), 97–110.
Hall, M. (2004) Reflexivity and tourism research. In J. Phillimore and L. Goodson (eds) *Qualitative Research in Tourism* (pp. 137–155). London: Routledge.
Kuang, L. (2001) *Study on the Tourism Industry Government Led Development Strategy.* Beijing: China Tourism Press.
Lin, Y. (1936) *My Country and My People.* London: William Heinemann.
Tribe, J. (2001) Research paradigms and the tourism curriculum. *Journal of Travel Research* 39, 442–448.
Tribe, J. (2006) The truth about tourism. *Annals of Tourism Research* 33 (2), 360–381.
Wearing, S. and Wearing, B. (2001) Conceptualising the selves of tourism. *Leisure Studies* 20, 143–159.

Appendix

This appendix provides a short list (including a brief introduction) of major reference sources of tourism research and industrial development as produced by CASS, CNTA and CTA.

Chinese Academy of Social Sciences (CASS)

(1) *Green Book of China's Tourism* (Nos 1–13)

This series (also titled *China's Tourism Development: Analysis and Forecast*) is one of the two flagship products of the Tourism Research Centre at the Chinese Academy of Social Sciences, which comprehensively discusses a wide variety of topics around tourism development in China. The chapters have been contributed by tourism scholars and practitioners from all over the Greater China region. Frequently discussed topics include market development, reform and innovation, highlights of the industry and tourism development in Hong Kong, Macau and Taiwan. The series has been published by the *Social Sciences Academic Press* since 2000. The 13th book in the series was published in 2015.

(2) *Green Book of China's Leisure* (Nos 1–3)

This series (also titled *Annual Report on China's Leisure Development*) is the other flagship product of the Tourism Research Centre at CASS. Similarly, this series discusses various topics related to leisure development in China, such as cultural leisure, sports and hot-spring spas. While this title reports on recent leisure research findings, overall it consists of practice-based industry reports. Like the *Green Book of China's Tourism*, this title is also a commissioned publication contributed to by scholars and practitioners both from CASS and from external institutions within the Greater China region. The series has been published by the *Social Sciences Academic Press* since 2011. The third book in the series was published in 2013.

China National Tourism Administration (CNTA)

The China National Tourism Administration, as the central government agency specialising in tourism administration in China, is mainly responsible for releasing national tourism statistics and general reports, namely *The Yearbook of China Tourism Statistics, The Tourist Survey Data* and *The Yearbook of China Tourism*. All three sources are published by the China Tourism Press in Beijing.

(1) *The Yearbook of China Tourism Statistics*

Starting in 1985, *The Yearbook of China Tourism Statistics* has been dedicated to presenting official tourism statistics, including an annual statistical bulletin giving details of the tourism industry and inbound arrivals, main features of inbound tourists, international tourism income, the general situation of domestic tourism, overnight inbound arrivals in different localities, the general situation of star-rated hotels, travel agencies, tourist attractions, and tourism enterprises and public institutions.

(2) *The Tourist Survey Data*

This series of publications originally concerned inbound tourists. In 2005 *The Inbound Tourist Survey Data (2005)* was released jointly by the Policy and Regulation Department of CNTA and the Urban Social and Economic Survey Team of the National Bureau of Statistics, representing the first publication of its kind in China. In 2006, *The Inbound Tourist Survey Data (2006)* and *The Domestic Tourist Survey Data (2006)* were published independently. This situation continued for the years of 2007 and 2008. In 2009, *The Tourist Survey Data* incorporating both domestic and inbound data were published. This practice has continued ever since. *The Tourist Survey Data* presents detailed survey data of inbound foreign tourists, compatriots from Hong Kong, Macau and Taiwan and domestic tourists in terms of their consumption amount and structure, length of stay, times of visitation and accommodation preferences.

(3) *The Yearbook of China Tourism*

From its first publication in 1990, *The Yearbook of China Tourism* has been dedicated to comprehensively displaying the current status and achievements of tourism development across the country as well as experts' viewpoints, government directives and policies, and leaders' speeches related to tourism development.

China Tourism Academy (CTA)

The China Tourism Academy, as the think-tank mainly for and affiliated to CNTA, has published (independently or jointly with departments of CNTA) the following annual editions of tourism and tourism development research.

(1) *China's Tourism Performance: Review and Forecast* (seven editions: 2008–2009, 2009–2010, 2010–2011, 2011–2012, 2012–2013, 2013–2014, 2014–2015)

Seven books in the *Blue Book of China's Tourism Economy* series have been published by the China Tourism Press since 2008. This series aims to provide state-of-the-art reports on CTA's research on the following issues: tourism economic monitoring and warnings, tourist satisfaction, hotel industry, travel agency, tourist attraction development, outbound and inbound tourism, and regional tourism development.

(2) *Annual Report of China Outbound Tourism Development* (seven editions: 2006, 2007 & 2008, 2009–2010, 2011, 2012, 2013, 2014)

Seven books in this series have been published by the China Tourism Press and the Tourism Education Press alternately since 2006. Since the 2007 & 2008 edition, this series has been chaired and edited by CTA (which was established in 2008). The series aims to provide state-of-the-art reports on CTA's research on China's outbound tourism development, including the following major issues: influencing factors, market status and regional distribution of China's outbound tourism, and Chinese outbound tourists' behaviour. The 2011, 2012, 2013 and 2014 editions had an independent English version.

(3) *Annual Report of China Inbound Tourism Development* (three editions: 2012, 2013, 2014)

Three reports in this series have been published by the Tourism Education Press since 2012. The annual report series is edited jointly by the Tourism

Promotion and International Cooperation Department of CNTA and CTA. It focuses on the uneven development of inbound tourism development in China and its market features.

(4) *Annual Report of China Regional Tourism Development* (four editions: 2010–2011, 2011–2012, 2012–2013, 2013–2014)

Four reports in this series have been published by the China Tourism Press and the Tourism Education Press alternately since 2011. The major purpose of this series is to provide a geographical overview of tourism development in China, including originating places development for tourism, tourism destination development, and tourist flows.

(5) *Annual Report of China Leisure Development* (three editions: 2011–2012, 2012–2013, 2013–2014)

The title is a newly added book series with a special focus on Chinese leisure development, covering the following important issues: Chinese residents' leisure behaviours, leisure-related companies' development, leisure industrial development, and trend analysis. Since the first book published in 2012, this series has been published by the Tourism Education Press in Beijing.

(6) *Annual Report of China Tourism Groups Development* (two editions: 2012, 2013)

This is a book series specialising in analysing tourism-related group companies' development in China. Important issues that have been covered include the investors, investment models and invested industries of tourism-related group companies. Each of the published two editions has a theme: *Tourism investment in China: investor, models and formats* (2012), and *Business research & development and independent innovation: a new driving force for the growth of China's tourism groups* (2013). This series is published by the Tourism Education Press in Beijing.

(7) *China Travel Agency Industry Development Annual Report* (three editions: 2012, 2013, 2014)

This is also a recently added book series with a special focus on the development of the travel agency industry in China, with the following important issues covered in different volumes: development history and evolution of the travel agency industry in China, the current state of this industry, behaviour of consumers organised by travel agencies, policy and regulations, and online travel agency development. Since the first book published in 2012, this series has been published by the China Tourism Press and the Tourism Education Press alternately.

(8) *China Tourism Scenic Development Report* (two editions: 2013, 2014)

The Chinese title for this series indicates that it is specifically dedicated to analysing the development of tourist attractions (scenic areas) in China. The major topics covered in the past two volumes include tourist demands and investment, and the performance and future trends of tourist attractions. The series has been published by the Tourism Education Press since 2013.

(9) *Development Report of China's Hotel Industry* (four editions: 2009, 2010–2011, 2012–2013, 2013–2014)

The four reports of this series have been published by the Tourism Education Press since 2010. Since the 2010–2011 edition, each of the published reports has focused on one specific topic. The 2010–2011 edition's topic was on hotel groups; the 2012–2013 edition's topic was hotel development and innovation; and the 2012–2013 edition concentrated on brand creation and format innovation.

(10) *China Tourism Review* (issues: 2011, 2012, 2013, 2014, Special issue on policy, No. 1, No. 2; 2015, No. 1)

This is actually a book series, published by the Tourism Education Press since 2011, which contains commissioned academic or practice-based papers on various issues related to tourism development in China. In 2014, three issues were published, including a special issue on tourism policy.

Index

For Product Safety Concerns and Information please contact our EU Authorised Representative:

Easy Access System Europe

Mustamäe tee 50

10621 Tallinn

Estonia

gpsr.requests@easproject.com

www.ingramcontent.com/pod-product-compliance
Ingram Content Group UK Ltd.
Pitfield, Milton Keynes, MK11 3LW, UK
UKHW021843280426

5452IPUK00003B/33

* 9 7 8 1 8 4 5 4 1 5 4 6 4 *